2/15

1

# The Tradition of Indian Architecture

# The Tradition of Indian Architecture

Continuity, Controversy and Change since 1850

G.H.R. Tillotson

Yale University Press
New Haven and London · 1989

Designed by Susan Rossen A.I.C.

Set in Linotron Bembo by
SX Composing Ltd, Rayleigh, Essex
Printed and bound in Hong Kong through
Bookbuilders Ltd

**Library of Congress Cataloging-in-Publication Data**
Tillotson, G. H. R. (Giles Henry Rupert), 1960-
    The tradition of Indian architecture:
  continuity, controversy and change
  since 1850 / by G. H. R. Tillotson.
       p.     cm.
    Bibliography: p.
    Includes index.
    ISBN 0-300-04636-7
    1. Architecture—India—British influences.  2. Architecture, Modern—19th century—India—British influences.  3. Architecture, Modern—20th century—India—British influences.  4. Architecture and state—India.  5. Architecture, Modern—20th century—India. I. Title.
NA 1503.T55   1990
720′,954-dc20                           89-33202
                                                 CIP

# Contents

Taxila

•Srinagar

Lahore• •Kapurthala

•Chandigarh

Bikaner    Delhi    Bulandshahr
•    Nawalgarh    •
Jaisalmer    Mathura    Agra    •Lucknow
•    Jaipur•    •    Cooch Behar
Jodhpur    Ajmer    Tonk    Gwalior    Allahabad
•    •    •    •    •Benares

Panna
•

Chandernagore
Sanchi
Ahmedabad    •    Bhopal    Calcutta
Morvi    •    Indore
Porbandar    Baroda    Mandu
Junagadh    •Surat    •Nagpur

Aurangabad
•
Bombay    I N D I A
Elephanta

•Hyderabad

•Kolhapur

•Goa

Bangalore    Madras
•    •
Mysore    Pondicherry
•    •
Tranquebar
Tanjore•
•Cochin

0    100    250 miles

# Preface

*We cannot get rid of the body of tradition, murder it how we may.*
Edwin Lutyens

Through the course of India's cultural history runs a theme of interaction. At least since the Aryan invasions of about 1500 BC, the country's vast land mass has been host to a plurality of cultural traditions, and at times different – sometimes fundamentally opposed – traditions have been brought into contact and something new has arisen. This book describes the most recent, and perhaps the most extreme, recurrence of the pattern: it is a study of the changes in India's architectural tradition and in Indian taste that occurred in response to the influence of British architecture in India and the policies of British imperial rule. It considers also the controversies that those changes stirred, for this interaction, so obviously critical to the future of Indian civilization, was attended by often vehement public debate. It is a study of part of the transformation of one civilization by another, and of prolonged crises of power, responsibility and identity.

In recent years, some valuable work has been done on British architecture in India. The present book does not repeat this work: though it discusses some colonial buildings, its primary concern is with their effects on the indigenous tradition. Some interesting work has also been done on the influence of Indian styles on the architecture of the West; the principal subject of this book could be said to be the opposite of that. The buildings that it describes are often more fascinating than beautiful, but they chart the progress of one of the most significant developments in the history of Indian culture, a development which is still in the process of resolution.

The treatment of the material is not entirely chronological. The first chapter covers the whole period of the nineteenth and early twentieth centuries, and describes the modification of traditional Indian design by the introduction of classical motifs, copied from colonial buildings. The second chapter covers the same historical period but considers another aspect of change, namely the revolution in taste and cultural alignment among India's native ruling classes, which gave rise to new habits of patronage. The central chapter focusses on the revival of traditional forms and methods in Indian architecture and crafts in the last two decades of the nineteenth century. The final two chapters bring the story up to date, firstly by assessing the impact of the building of New Delhi early in this century, and secondly by describing certain developments in India's architecture since Independence in 1947, including the building of Chandigarh. In no sense do these chapters amount to a complete history of Indian architecture since 1850; nor do they even give complete accounts of individual episodes, such as the development of New Delhi or of Lucknow: in each case, the emphasis of the discussion lies on the political motives that underlay the architectural designs, and on their critical reception.

In an effort to forestall misinterpretation, it may be worthwhile establishing two points at the outset. First, this is not a critique – nor any part of a critique – of colonialism. Its concern is to describe events in architectural history, not to evaluate political systems; and although many aspects of British influence on Indian architecture are here deplored, there has been no need – and no temptation – to draw comparisons with political life in India in the period of colonial rule. It would be rather late in the day to harangue British imperialism. Secondly, in spite of conspicuously siding with those who sought to defend India's native cultural traditions, this book is not a plea for the restoration of historicism in Indian architecture. Historicist approaches to design are now somewhat in vogue elsewhere, but no analogous movement for India is here proposed. Indeed, one of the book's central arguments seeks to distinguish historicism from continuity of tradition.

The field-work on which this study is based was funded by grants from the Master and Fellows of Peterhouse, and the Managers of the Smuts Memorial Fund. My work in India would have been much less enjoyable without the fabulous hospitality and kindness of Dr Manu Singhvi, his wife, Anita, and his parents, Dr and Mrs L.M. Singhvi – in fact, the entire Singhvi household. I am similarly grateful to Nimish Patel and Parul Zaveri, whose hospitality and conversation were an inspiration in many things. I should also like to thank Drs Bridget and Raymond Allchin, Dr Mildred Archer, Dr Asok Das, Nisha Grover, Dr Narayani Gupta, Dr J.C. Harle, Gillian Malpass, John Nicoll, Susan F. Rossen, Yaduendra Sahai, Andrew Topsfield and Dr John Twigg. My father-in-law, Professor Ian Glynn, has with customary patience improved my grammar, while my mother-in-law, Jenifer Glynn, improved my reasoning; I am very grateful to them both. I owe most, as always, to my wife, Sarah, who studied and discussed the subject with me throughout, and whose formative contribution cannot be measured.

G.H.R.T.
Cambridge, July 1988

CHAPTER ONE

# 'An Unsuccessful Attempt at the Grecian'

When the English topographical artists Thomas and William Daniell arrived in Calcutta early in 1786, they set about producing a series of engravings depicting the city's colonial buildings. They were anxious, even then, to leave Calcutta and travel up country in order to see something of India's native architectural heritage, but before they could afford such a venture they were obliged to concentrate on the subjects that Calcutta had to offer. A colonial city, it contained little for those in quest of indigenous design, but the Daniells sought out the native quarter known as Chitpore and sketched its few remarkable buildings. They knew that they were not seeing the best of Indian architecture, as is apparent from Thomas's comments on a house which features in a later aquatint (fig. 1):

> In this view on the Chitpore road . . . appears the house of a native
> Bengal merchant; the style of architecture in its ornamental parts is
> Mahommedan, except in the turret, which is an unsuccessful attempt at
> the Grecian, as introduced by the Portugueze. These incongruities very
> frequently occur in modern Indian buildings, whose owners have
> intercourse with Europeans.[1]

Daniell attributed the influence to the Portuguese because they were the earliest colonists in India and had been building since the mid-sixteenth century. Vasco da Gama had reached India in 1498; and in 1510 Albuquerque took Goa and so established a Portuguese colony which was subsequently embellished with churches and other alien structures. It is more likely, though, that the models on which the Chitpore house drew were those closer to hand: the British buildings of Calcutta.

Similar effects could be observed near other colonial settlements. Not long after Daniell commented on the process in Chitpore, a Hindu ruler at the other end of the subcontinent, Raja Sarabhoji of Tanjore (r. 1798-1832), ordered an extension to his palace in an attempted classical style.[2] It was perhaps this palace that arrested the attention of the art historian James Fergusson, who found in Tanjore a building

1. *View on the Chitpore Road, Calcutta,* aquatint by Thomas and William Daniell (1797).

made up of Italian balusters, some attenuated, some stumpy, intermixed with pillars and pilasters of the most hideous shapes, but all meant for Italian, and mixed up with Hindoo gods and goddesses, and little scraps of native Architecture peeping out here and there, so as to make up a whole so inexpressibly ludicrous and bad, that one hardly knows whether to laugh or be angry.[3]

The source of inspiration for the classical features of this chimera might have been the British buildings of Madras, or – less impressive but much closer by – the buildings of the Danish colony at Tranquebar, which had been founded on land granted to the Danes by an ancestor of Sarabhoji's in 1620.

The hybrids at Chitpore and Tanjore are not the earliest instances of European influence on Indian architecture. Following Alexander the Great's invasion of the north-western region in 326 BC, some classical motifs appeared in the architecture of Gandhara. The Corinthian pilasters of the Shrine of the Double-headed Eagle at Taxila (c. first century BC) are striking examples; but the trend did not last. More lasting contact with the Western world was established much later, in the Mughal period. This contact had profound effects on some Mughal

2

P3

art, especially painting, but little effect on architecture. Some *pietra dura* work of Italian style may be seen behind the throne of the principal hall of audience in the mid-seventeenth-century Mughal Red Fort in Delhi. Some of the panels are evidently original Italian work, imported complete, while their setting includes some Indian imitation of them. In the past, much was made of the European influence that these panels were supposed to signify (and they partly gave rise to the long-popular misconception that all Mughal inlay-work, including that on the Taj Mahal, is Italian in inspiration). In fact, the influence they do signify is very limited: they form a minor (though gorgeous) ornament in an unshakeably Indian hall.[4] The buildings described by Daniell and Fergusson indicate a more pervasive European influence.

*The Classical Models*

The classical models on which such experiments could draw were many and widespread: by the end of the seventeenth century, India's fringes were scattered with European settlements. On the west coast, the Portuguese were joined early in that century by the Dutch, operating through such ports as Surat and Cochin. A little later, on the Coromandel coast, the Danes at Tranquebar were joined by the British who founded Fort St. George (Madras) in 1644, and the French who founded Pondicherry in 1674. At the end of the century, the European traders reached the north-east corner of the subcontinent: the French founded Chandernagore around 1690, and the British founded Fort William (Calcutta) in 1696.

These foreign settlements soon contained a great range of building types. The variety of structures included the industrial, such as factories and docks; the military, such as forts and barracks; the residential, from private houses to governors' palaces; and the religious, with monuments and tombs as well as churches. With the growth of political power and administration, this range was augmented by official buildings, including courts, mints and town halls. What all these buildings had in common was their architectural vocabulary: the overwhelming majority of colonial buildings constructed in India before the mid-nineteenth century were designed in classical styles. Among the earliest of them were the sixteenth-century Portuguese forts at Daman and Diu, the Cathedral of Bom Jesus built in Goa in 1594 (fig. 2), St. Mary's Church in Madras (consecrated in 1680), and the mid-eighteenth-century French Government Houses in Pondicherry and Chandernagore.

By the time the Daniells arrived in Calcutta, that city already contained many considerable buildings, some of which formed the subjects of the engravings that they issued there in their first two years of residence. These buildings include the Old Court House, built about 1756; the Old Government House on Esplanade Row, built in 1767; the Writers' Building, built in 1780; and St. John's Church, which the Daniells saw being completed in 1787 to the designs of James Agg (fig. 3).

2. Old Goa; Bom Jesus
Basilica (1594).

Though few are entirely without dignity, these early colonial buildings are not among the finest examples of European architectural design. Even their most enthusiastic admirers concede that they are frequently derivative of more ambitious projects in the parent countries. This is partly because they were designed not architects but by military engineers whose training had taught them more about fortifications that about civil architecture. In the early trading days, architecture was not a high priority: if the engineer who was on site could put up something serviceable, the early colonists were content. Through habit, this pattern persisted even after the potential political power of architecture had been discerned. The military engineers depended on books to fill the gaps in their training: many a British building in India was assembled from the pages of Colin Campbell's *Vitruvius Britannicus*, or from the publications of Stuart and Revett, William Chambers and the Adams. St. John's Church in Calcutta was among the earliest of a large number of British churches in India to be based (rather roughly in this case) on James Gibbs's designs for St. Martin-in-the-Fields, designs which had been published by Gibbs in *A Book of Architecture* of 1728. Many engineers, though, preferred less stimulating inspiration and opted for a bland Palladianism. Little can honestly be said for the results. It was perhaps in an effort to retain some buoyancy for his chosen subject that Sten Nilsson was so generous to Thomas Lyon's Writers' Building as to describe its original facade as 'almost dull'.[5]

4

3. *St. John's Church,* aquatint by Thomas and William Daniell (1788).

It was mostly from such buildings – scarcely the best models to study – that Indian architects derived their knowledge of the classical tradition. In some instances, the colonists did not stop at providing poor models for imitation, but actively taught bad classicism. Some of the early Dutch and English traders operating in Ahmedabad and Surat, for example, wanting to construct tombs for themselves, and wanting these to be in a Western style, but (as traders rather than architects) being unable to remember fully the details of the classical orders, gave imperfect and incomplete instructions to the local native masons. In the absence of coherent direction, the masons' own traditions partly reasserted themselves. The seventeenth-century Dutch tombs in Ahmedabad and the Oxinden family mausoleum in Surat consequently mix Indian design with inexact classicism. Similarly, the early Portuguese brought no architects with them, so that when they began to build their great cathedrals the work was done by native masons supervised by priests. The many errors against the classical canon that these buildings perpetrate suggest that the Indian masons, quite ignorant of classical design, received their instruction from Europeans barely less ignorant.

Around 1800, British architecture in India received a major new impetus. It was not that there was any marked rise in the quality of design, but there was a decided rise in pretentiousness. The new Government Houses in Calcutta and Madras were intended to reflect the princely pretentions of a new breed of nabob. That in Calcutta, built between 1799 and 1803 on the orders of the Marquess Wellesley, was so lavish that it was a consideration in the recall of Wellesley. Yet its design was entrusted, as usual, to an engineer who based his plans on an existing building in England: Lt. Charles Wyatt adhered closely to the model of Kedleston Hall in Derbyshire (of which the original plans by James Paine had been published in 1783). The rebuilding of the Government House in Madras between 1800 and 1802, with the addition of a vast Banqueting Hall, was similarly entrusted to an engineer, John Goldingham.

These two palaces, though on a grander scale than anything the British colonists had built before, were still geographically peripheral. But at the same time, the British began to present a more princely image of themselves at two of the most powerful native courts in India: Lucknow in the north and Hyderabad in the south. In each place, the local ruler was persuaded to pay for a palace to house his British representative. The Lucknow Residency was begun in 1780 and much extended around 1800; that at Hyderabad was built in 1803 to designs by Lt. Samuel Russell, under the scrutiny of its first occupant, James Achilles Kirkpatrick. These were British classical palaces built not on the margins but at the core of traditional royal India.

A consequence of the new impetus and purpose of British building in India was that, after 1800, the interpolation of classical details in native buildings became much more common, and it was no longer restricted to areas close to the colonial coastal settlements. One of the most striking early examples of this process is afforded by the architecture of Lucknow.


## Lucknow

Lucknow was for a little under a century the capital of Oudh (Avadh), during which time it was embellished with buildings by its Muslim rulers. The district of Oudh had formed part of the Mughal Empire, and in 1722 a Persian merchant named Sa'adat Khan Burhan-ul-Mulk was appointed its governor. This man served also as Wazir of the Empire, and he was succeeded in both posts by his son-in-law Safdar Jang (r. 1739-53), who established control over Oudh for a family dynasty. Safdar Jang was succeeded by his son, Shuja-ud-daulah (r. 1753-75). As Mughal power declined, the rulers of Lucknow were able to assert increasing autonomy (although they still styled themselves 'Nawab' or 'governor'); and eventually Oudh became the major seat of Islamic power in northern India, eclipsing Delhi. Shuja-ud-daulah's son and successor, Asaf-ud-daulah (r. 1775-97), marked the start of his reign by shifting his capital from Faizabad to Lucknow, on a bend on the Gumti River, and he began to build its palaces, tombs and mosques. The treaties which the Nawabs subsequently made with the British surrendered to the foreigners much of their power, for which they were recompensed with the title 'King'. In time, however, the

British grew tired of the Nawabs; they began to accuse them of incompetence and dissoluteness, and finally deposed the last of them, Wajid Ali Shah, in 1856.

The style of most of the major buildings constructed by the Nawabs of Lucknow, including all of the early ones, may be described as debased Mughal. In the major buildings of Asaf-ud-daulah, for example – the Bara Imambara, the Rumi Darwaza and the mosque between them (fig. 4) – the individual architectural forms employed are those that appear in mature Mughal buildings, but their treatment has dramatically altered, and in ways which serve to diminish rather than to enhance their power. Thus the cusped or foliated arches, the onion domes, the tapering minarets, the small domed kiosks or *chattris*, and many other features, all have their prototypes in the Mughal architecture of the preceding century; but they are here deployed in a new, less skilful manner.

There are several aspects to this decline. In mature Mughal architecture – such as that of Shah Jahan (r. 1627-58) – lavish surface ornament is spread over a firm structure; but here, the formerly robust outlines have been attenuated, so that the buildings are elegant but etiolated. Some individual forms are made smaller and multiplied in number: so, whereas in Mughal buildings a few isolated *chattris* may give emphasis at corners and other chosen points, here we more often

4. Lucknow; the mosque of Asaf-ud-daulah with the Rumi Darwaza beyond, seen from the roof of the Bara Imambara (1775-97).

7

have a continuous (seemingly endless) row of tiny *chattris*, an accentless fringe; and a similar effect is achieved by the long rows of tiny, arched openings which run around the edges of buildings, like the perforations of a postage stamp. We cannot even say that ornament has taken command, since although many details have become florid – the cusped arches break out in a vegetable extravagance – the rich quality and colour of Mughal ornament are gone: in place of inlaid semi-precious stones we have stucco froth. The major building materials are also shoddy: brick and stucco have replaced the Mughals' sandstone and marble. Some of the buildings are on a massively inflated scale, as if power could be expressed only through size. The main hall of the Bara Imambara measures 163 by 53 feet and stands nearly 50 feet high, but the size merely exaggerates the monotony of the facades, just as the cascade of steps before the mosque makes its feeble facade appear all the more theatrical.

Of course, this transition did not occur suddenly. The origins of the decline can be discerned even in late Mughal buildings such as the Bibi-ka-Maqbara at Aurangabad (1678); and the attenuation of outline and florid detailing are well established in the tomb of the early Nawab Wazir, Safdar Jang, in Delhi (c. 1753). The buildings of Lucknow, by further trivialising architectural forms and showing lower standards of finish and decoration, continue a decline begun elsewhere.

While the architects of Lucknow were thus attempting to sustain a stylistic tradition which was effectively already spent, and were in fact debasing it further by their experiments, they were suddenly presented with a new source of ideas. They were introduced to classical architecture through the buildings constructed by Europeans first in Bengal and soon in Lucknow itself. The Residency, as already mentioned, was begun around 1780 and developed over a long period, a banqueting hall and other detached houses being added in its grounds. Even in its heyday, though, the Residency was surpassed in splendour by Constantia (fig. 5). This palace on the edge of the city was built as the home and mausoleum of General Claude Martin, a French adventurer who served the East India Company and subsequently also the Nawabs.

Constantia was begun in 1795 and completed after Martin's death in 1800; part of the fortune he had amassed endowed a school which still occupies the building, now known in his memory as La Martinière. Impressive and ungainly, it is a large pyramidal structure, whose design is generally attributed to Martin himself.[6] Some of the details – especially the statuary – are extravagant, but the building is not at all what it has often been called, a stylistic hybrid.[7] To be sure, the battlements on the west front are an unusual feature in a classical design (their presence may be explained by Martin's obsession with military affairs[8]), but they are not uncanonical. The domed kiosks on the roof perhaps faintly recall Indian *chattris*, but the forms they employ – the columns and arches – are purely classical. Such kiosks may have no basis in classical archaeology, but they are scarcely more fanciful (even if less happy) than, say, the roofline devised by

5. Lucknow; Constantia
(begun 1795).

Vanbrugh for Blenheim Palace. Constantia is notable less for being a hybrid
than for being an example of amateurish and slightly incompetent classicism. Its
transgressions against the rules of Palladian art were noted by Fergusson, and
Nilsson commented with characteristic mildness: 'The series of orders is extremely unconventional: three Composites above a Tuscan. And in the central
tower single pilasters support half–columns in pairs with heavy cornices; this
arrangement is contrary to all classicist functional theory.'[9]

Constantia and the Residency exerted a potent influence on the subsequent
architecture of Lucknow.[10] Both buildings were most probably constructed by a
native labour force, working under European direction;[11] and by this procedure,
the craftsmen who built the Nawabs' palaces and tombs received an unexpected
education in classical design. The already continuing decline of the native style
shows that Lucknow's architects were not notably inventive; they must therefore have been delighted to be given a new, ready-made repertoire of motifs,
and certainly many of the buildings produced in Lucknow after 1800 incorporate
classical forms. It is true that the debased Mughal style which characterizes the
buildings of the early Nawabs was sustained even to the end of the Nawabi
period, in such buildings as the Chota (Husainabad) Imambara (1837) and the

9

6. Lucknow; Kaisarbagh gate (1848-50).

Jami Masjid (begun in 1840); but these buildings, by being free of European forms, are exceptions to the general development after 1800. Most late Nawabi buildings exemplify a hybrid style in which classical forms are inserted into the Indian scheme, a style which mixes Indian cusped with classical round arches, *chattris* with pediments, *chajjas* (or Indian dripstones) with string-courses, Mughal balustered columns with classical columns and pilasters.

An early and tentative essay in this hybrid style is found in the tombs of Sa'a-dat Ali Khan (d. 1814) and his wife. These tombs follow Indian tradition in their form and almost every detail, but have oval lights in the domes (which are all the more startling for being unique foreign features). The experiment was evidently considered a success, for it was repeated in the tomb of Sa'adat Ali Khan's successor, Ghazi-ud-din Haidar (d. 1827).[12] The Chattar Manzil, the palace built by Nasir-ud-din-Haidar (r. 1827-37), deploys classical columns and arches over its facades more boldly.

The most ambitious project in the hybrid style, however, was the Kaisarbagh. Originally an extensive palace complex, it has lost some parts; what remains are the ranges surrounding a large, open, rectangular space, entered by

10

gates on the north-west and south-east sides. These gates and ranges were built by the last Nawab, Wajid Ali Shah, in 1848-50. In each of the gates (fig. 6), the openings are round arches contained within cusped arches. The stucco-work above the inner arch similarly shows European influence, and the superstructure was originally decked out with European statues and crowns.[13] The strange skeletal dome, made of curved brackets, is copied from Constantia. These European forms consort with Indian domes and balconies and some traditional plaster-work. The *chajja* hesitates between the two traditions – it projects horizontally as if to resemble a classical cornice – while the flanking ranges have made up their minds to be purely classical. If the Kaisarbagh gates are still essentially Indian with European features, the formula is reversed in the gate of the Sikandarbagh, built by the same ruler (fig. 7). This is a predominantly classical composition, though the classical forms are somewhat unconventionally grouped, and they are capped by an Indian roofline.

In design, such buildings stand at a considerable remove from the original Lucknow style – that of early buildings such as the Bara Imambara. The mature Mughal style, from which that early Lucknow style was derived, had itself been

11

the result of a fusion between two distinct architectural traditions, the one indigenous and Hindu, the other imported and Islamic. Typically, Mughal buildings take from the Islamic tradition the technology of arcuate construction, the form of the pointed arch, and simple geometrical planning and massing, while inheriting from the Hindu tradition a propensity for rich stone carving, and trabeate construction with some of its attendant forms, including corbels. In later Mughal buildings especially (such as the pavilions of Shah Jahan's palaces in Agra and Delhi), these elements of disparate origin are not merely mixed but bound together in a new architectural logic. The synthesis of the two traditions is emphasized by a considerable use of forms which had been developed in both Hindu and Islamic buildings in India, and so which cannot be classified as distinctly of one denomination or the other. Such forms are the cusped arch, the curved or *bangaldar* roof and the *chajja*. All have ancient Indian antecedents and prototypes in the great medieval Hindu temples, but in later times they were developed also in Islamic buildings in India; so that, when they were at last adopted in Mughal buildings, their origins were but faint echoes, and they had shed exclusive cultural associations. As a result, Mughal architecture presents a new style, distinct from Islamic architecture elsewhere and from its Hindu sources, though visibly derived from both. It is, above all, a resolved style.

By the time it was redeployed in the early buildings of Lucknow, this style, as already recounted, was somewhat debased. With the appearance in Lucknow of classical models, however, a further synthesis was attempted, this time between the flagging Mughal style and the new immigrant, classical design. But the result, though often called a synthesis,[14] is in fact never anything more than a mixture. Classical forms were hastily adopted with no long evolution over time, no joint working out of forms, such as had occurred in the earlier instance. The details of classical architecture – its columns, pediments and arches – were not developed or changed into something new (except by inexact copying). They were inserted into Indian designs, apparently with no sense that these forms were part of a language of architecture which had evolved over centuries – a language which, like any other, has its own conventions and usages which must be respected (or at least known, so that if they are to be defied, as by a mannerist or a modernist, they can be defied with wit and intelligence). In the hands of Lucknow's architects, classical architecture became not a grammar but a box of novelties with which to trick out a building. They picked up its forms without comprehending their intrinsic significance or historical development.

There is a long tradition of European critical assault on the buildings of Lucknow. Much of this criticism is simply scornful, though even then it is often based on the serious ground that the architects failed to understand and consequently abused classicism. It was just this ground that motivated the early and thoughtful critic James Fergusson. Fergusson was aware that, in such buildings as Constantia, the architects of Lucknow had the worst models to work from, but he also realised that this was only part of the problem:

Of course no native of India can well understand either the origin of motive of the various parts of our Orders – why the entablature should be divided in architrave, frieze and cornice – why the shafts should be a certain number of diameters in height, and so on. It is, in fact, like a man trying to copy an inscription in a language he does not understand, and of which he does not even know the alphabet. With the most correct eye and the greatest pains he cannot do it accurately.[15]

Such reflections led him to lament the introduction of classicism into India as 'an unmitigated misfortune. The unintelligent vulgarity with which the "Orders" are there used, by a people who were capable of such noble things in their own styles, is one of the most startling phenomena in the history of architecture.'[16] Fergusson singled out, as an example of 'unintelligent vulgarity', the Kaisar-bagh palace, where 'Italian windows with Venetian blinds alternate with Saracenic arcades, or openings of no style whatever.'[17]

But it is not only Europeans with a classical education who have deplored the later developments in Lucknow architecture. The late nineteenth-century Urdu essayist Abdul Halim Sharar commended the early buildings such as the Bara Imambara for being free of European influence, but noticed a decline from the reign of Sa'adat Ali Khan: 'Unfortunately, having lived in Calcutta and Benares he had been introduced to a variety of architectural styles, and his taste had become so vitiated that buildings constructed in his time are devoid of the old flavour'.[18]

More recently, however, Nawabi architecture has found some ardent defenders. Courageously, they have quoted from the fusillade of abuse that has been directed against the buildings (and much of which is enviably witty and apt). They have told us that for the hundred years following the demise of the Nawabs, the combination of European and Indian features found in their buildings was described by such phrases as 'not without a grotesque grace'[19] or 'cheerfully indiscriminate'.[20] The apologists have quoted such views to illustrate what they suppose is revealed about the commentators, forgetting that comments sometimes in addition reveal something about the thing commented on. And so they have not felt called on to address the point that underlies much of the abuse, and that was first argued in earnest by Fergusson, namely, that the mixed-style Nawabi buildings are bad because they defy traditions without understanding them, that they are architecturally illiterate. One defender has described the mixture at the Kaisarbagh as 'the Nawabi style at its zenith', and concluded that the mixed style in general is 'an enduring and aesthetically valid legacy for north Indian art throughout the 19th and early 20th centuries'.[21] Another has quoted Fergusson's comments and, ignoring entirely the argument they express, accused him of 'patronising amusement' and 'narrowness of vision'.[22] It is, perhaps, unwise to take on Fergusson, a man who was astonishingly well versed in both Indian and Western traditions and who was therefore well placed to assess

13

the architecture of Lucknow. The charge of narrowness is absurd when levelled against one who wrote with understanding on architecture throughout the world, and who knew better than his detractor the merits of the Indian tradition when not adulterated by European influence.

Underlying such charges of narrowness and complaints about 'purists who were affronted at buildings which challenged conventional notions',[23] is an exhortation to broaden our frames of reference, to judge things on their own merits. We are told that we require an 'understanding of the forces which shaped Lucknow's buildings',[24] that we should see things in their context. The issue not settled is the form that our broad-mindedness should take. Certainly, if we are to admire any Eastern architecture, or even understand it as its designers intended, we must exercise a cultural pluralism. What this pluralism means is the assessment of works of art according to an appropriate aesthetic canon: it is the recognition that each of the world's various architectural traditions has evolved under the guidance of a distinct aesthetic canon, and that we must be acquainted with that canon if we are to assess fairly. So, it would be absurd to expect a Chinese or Indian building to conform to Greek systems of proportion. Such pluralism is perhaps more customary in other fields. Considered as dogs, most cats are regrettably deficient; but rational people, when considering cats, invoke feline not canine criteria, however much they love dogs. Nonetheless, the same clear thought is not always found in art-historical writing of the past: many Westerners have indeed carried the canon of the Parthenon east of Athens, and found Oriental pagodas deficient by comparison. Fergusson was not one such: when he made comparisons between East and West, it was to demonstrate the divergence of aims.[25] He knew that in the assessment of Indian buildings, Indian criteria apply. To be sure, he assumed that some criteria (including notions of propriety to materials) were common to all cultures, but he knew that in each civilization many (and especially those concerning proportion and decoration) were unique.

Cultural pluralism of this kind is essential if we are to examine Eastern art, for what it amounts to is a knowledge of the aesthetic ideals that guided the artists. What is not necessary is that we should so broaden our minds as to suspend all judgement altogether; that we should admit the bad as well as the good, denying ourselves the right to distinguish between them. Relativism renders criticism pointless; but avoiding that snare need not entail adopting an absolutist stand: between those positions is that of the pluralist who recognizes a range of objective standards. While it is absurdly unjust to dismiss works of art as bad when they fail according to some arbitrarily chosen aesthetic, it is not absurd to do so if they fail according to their own local aesthetic.

What, then, is the case with the mixed-style buildings of Lucknow? As they draw on two established architectural traditions, we cannot but assess them in those two contexts. And whether we assess them as classical or as Islamic design, they fail, for both traditions are clumsily (not cleverly) defied. And since these traditions are mixed rather than fused, the buildings do not establish (as Mughal buildings do) an aesthetic of their own by which we might assess them. Indeed, their hybrid character pours scorn on the very notion of an aesthetic canon, of an architectural tradition – and it is for just this reason that they have themselves been scorned.

It is significant in this context that one defender of Nawabi architecture has argued that the European influence is often very superficial, affecting only '"non-essential" features' and surface ornament.[26] The classical or neo-classical architect would be surprised to see some of the features that are borrowed – and notably the column – referred to as 'non-essential'. In classical architecture, the column is the essence; but in Lucknow, where it is one among a number of novel embellishments, it is indeed treated as 'non-essential'. Such usage, according to this defender, should offend no one but 'the European purist'; and another admirer has similarly derided the 'purists' who are unreceptive to 'a latent vitality and creative element'.[27] The charge of purism, so easily levied, is yet so satisfyingly potent, sending the conservative and the academic snob scuttling for cover. But it is one thing to assert that an architectural style must never be changed by time or external influence (a purism few would espouse); it is another to deplore the reduction of an established architectural grammar to a sourcebook of decorations, the reduction of the classical orders to '"non-essential" features'. If, in our interpretation of architecture, we jettison our knowledge of tradition, we are left with little. We still have the form, but half the meaning is gone.

Some of the early criticism of Lucknow architecture is based not on considerations such as those above; less perspicacious than Fergusson's, it is based on a fundamental confusion about architectural expression, as Rosie Llewellyn-Jones has demonstrated.[28] In the last century, the Nawabs of Lucknow were widely perceived as dissolute and incapable, and it was alleged by some of the early critics that the evident decadence of Nawabi architecture was a reflection of the decadence of the court; for they supposed that architecture is always in some way, principally and by necessity, an embodiment of the age that produces it. They transferred a part of their contempt for the people to the architecture: expecting buildings always to reveal the character of their creators, they confounded moral with aesthetic judgements.

This view of architecture as primarily a lithic expression of an age or a political regime is a habit widespread among the English (though not peculiar to them); it is by no means restricted to nineteenth-century comments about Lucknow. It is a sort of architectural pathetic fallacy. Since it is still current (and more often assumed than considered),[29] it may be worthwhile to point out some of its limitations. In the first place, it offers a very incomplete account of architecture. While one may on occasion find an analogy between an architectural design and some political circumstance of its time, that analogy will not form a complete description of the design. The pomposity of Versailles may be taken to reflect the pomposity of Louis XIV, but Versailles represents also (among other things) a particular moment in the development of French Baroque classicism, a development in architectural style which has little to do with Louis's personality. Secondly, any connection that does exist between a design and its political era, exists as a matter of fact rather than of compulsion or necessity. There is no sound logical ground for insisting that a court (whether decadent or virile) is bound to promote architecture that mirrors its own character.[30] When buildings do reveal something of the characters of their builders or their age, they do so not inevitably, but because there was some mechanism by which the political circumstance informed what architects drew. The European stylistic influence in Lucknow buildings is certainly a reflection of (because it was occasioned by) a European political influence; but their weakness and clumsiness cannot be read as a reflection of similar qualities in the Nawabs (even supposing the implied judgement on the Nawabs were fair), because there was no mechanism by which such a reflection could have been achieved.

It is worth pointing out, in passing, that the political analogy is no more serviceable when turned to the defence of Nawabi architecture. It might be argued, for example, that if the buildings are uncertain or unresolved, then this is forgivable since they were produced in uncertain times.[31] Such a defence would, of course, entail the same pathetic fallacy: there is no intrinsic reason why architecture must express a given political instability. The early years of the reign of the Mughal Emperor Akbar (r. 1556-1605) were an unstable, turbulent period, which nevertheless produced some of the most confident designs of Mughal architecture, including Humayun's tomb. By contrast, the reign of his son Jahangir (1605-27), resting on the foundations laid by the father, was a comparatively stable period, but the major Jahangiri buildings – including the tombs of Akbar, Itimad-ud-daulah and Jahangir himself – are curiously unresolved and devoid of the former vigour of outline. The disjunction in these cases between the prevailing political spirit of an age and its architecture demonstrates that the connection, even where it exists, is not inevitable. So one cannot logically defend a bad design by saying that it had to be so because the times were bad.

Apart from its lack of logic, such a defence reduces art history to a sort of handicap competition. It springs, no doubt, from a desire to be even-handed in assessment. But while we might reasonably feel bound to evaluate buildings in terms of a relevant aesthetic canon, we need not feel bound to find some justification for each and every design. We need not suppose that it is only possible to describe a work of art as bad if we have failed to understand some aspect of the circumstances in which it was produced. Some works are bad, even when appraised by appropriate criteria, and saying so is a proper occupation for the art historian. (It is hoped that all these remarks on method will not be considered otiose; they may even be essential in an essay that is replete with aesthetic judgements, written in a country where the interpretation of art is chiefly iconographical.)

The Lucknow apologists have two remaining lines of defence. One is to ask rhetorically whose fault it all is: it is all very well, they imply, for European critics to despise Lucknow's architecture, but it was Europeans who introduced the debilitating influence. Apart from modern writers,[32] Abdul Halim Sharar pursued this line: with his customary elegant restraint, he remarked that Europeans deplored the buildings of his city, and that 'they said that the local style was ruined because it had no strong tradition, but no one gave a thought as to who had ruined it. "O morning breeze. All this has been brought about by thee"'.[33] It is, of course, true that Europeans provided the models to copy, but identifying the accessory does not eradicate the fact of the deed. That Europeans were ultimately to blame does not make the buildings any better.

Finally, it is argued that the interpolation and distortion of classical forms found in Nawabi buildings is analogous to the treatment of Indian forms found in some buildings of Georgian Britain; the Lucknow mixed style is compared to that brief vogue for Indian things which reached its zenith in the Royal Pavilion at Brighton, as remodelled by John Nash between 1815 and 1818.[34] There is some substance to this comparison, for both fashions involve the misunderstanding and misapplication of a foreign tradition adopted for its exotic appeal. But in making the comparison, the Lucknow apologists surrender all claim for their wards to be considered as great – or even serious – architecture. And they overlook certain differences between the two fashions. The Royal Pavilion is not an attempt at a faithful imitation of Indian forms. Georgian Indianism was usually (and especially in Nash's case) based on a very slight knowledge of the original, and the very remoteness of the supposedly Indian features from the original models shows that what was intended was not copying, but something more like parody (though the remoteness removes its sting). The Royal Pavilion is not a near miss at Indian architecture, it is a fantasy on Indian architecture: the Indian forms are distorted not through imprecise copying but through invention. And the invention is consciously whimsical, deliberately absurd, and brilliant. The Lucknow architects aimed to copy classical forms faithfully and got them wrong (for the variety of reasons already outlined); their parody of classicism was unintentional.[35]

Furthermore, the Royal Pavilion is one among a small number of such caprices. The Indian style in England briefly enjoyed great popularity, but it was never part of the mainstream development of British architecture. It was dropped as abruptly as it had been taken up, and was not considered (then or since) as an 'enduring and aesthetically valid legacy'. In India, the imitation of classical forms was the major architectural development of the mid-nineteenth century. The number and the geographical range of the examples make a difference in quantity which amounts to a difference in kind.

## Rajasthan

For though Lucknow was one of the first, it was not the only Indian royal capital to be affected by European influence in this way. The influence soon became widespread, driving out traditional local design. Fergusson lamented this general development in 1875, commending the regions not yet touched by it:

> No one who has personally visited the objects of interest with which India abounds can fail to be struck with the extraordinary elegance of detail and propriety of design which pervades all the architectural achievements of the Hindus; and this not only in buildings erected in former days, but in those now in course of construction in those parts of the country to which the bad taste of their European rulers has not yet penetrated.[36]

But even as he wrote, the number of unpenetrated parts of the country was rapidly decreasing, and before the end of the century, the European influence had broached the last surviving stronghold of traditional Indian design, Rajasthan. Not that any resistance was offered; indeed, the classical style was welcomed like a Trojan horse. For just as Nawabi architecture of the late eighteenth century represents a decline from the standards of Mughal design, so the eighteenth-century buildings of Rajasthan are etiolated versions of the great Rajput palaces built between the fifteenth and seventeenth centuries; and again the contact with Western civilization put at the Rajasthani designers' disposal a whole new repertoire of forms. The round arch and round column, the fanlight and the pediment became their special favourites, and they attempted through a judicious insertion of these novelties to inject new life into their visibly flagging tradition.

Three hundred miles west of Lucknow, in eastern Rajasthan, lay another Islamic kingdom with a line of nawabs. While Lucknow was a powerful state in a geographically commanding position, Tonk was small, remote and of next to no political significance; but their later architectural history followed the same pattern. Towards the end of the nineteenth century, the Nawab of Tonk added to his palace a detached, two-storeyed pavilion known as the Sunehri Kothi (fig. 8). In its essentials, this pavilion is typical of the palace architecture of the region: the complex division of internal spaces, and the lavish decoration in the main upper chamber repeat long-established local themes. But amid the traditional decorative techniques – the inlaid coloured glass, painted plaster, and mirror-work – we find some flower paintings evidently copied from Western prints, banal as birthday cards. On the exterior, the European influence is registered in the *trompe-l'oeil* marbling of the columns on the upper storey, and the imitation Ionic columns with painted fluting below. *Trompe-l'oeil* devices are not traditional in India, but they contain an element of ingenuity that is often a part of the appeal of a novelty, and so it is not surprising to find them adopted here. Some of this building's doors are painted illusions and must have given the

8. Tonk; Sunehri Kothi (late nineteenth century).

9. Jaipur; a house front on Johari Bazaar (late nineteenth century).

Nawab occasions to laugh at those of his courtiers who were not initiated into clever Western trickery.

Tonk's neighbours in Rajasthan were the Hindu states ruled by the Rajput maharajas: immediately to the north, for example, lay the kingdom of the Kach-

19

waha rulers. In 1727, the Kachwahas had transferred their capital from the old citadel of Amber to the newly built city of Jaipur. Coming late in the development of Rajput architecture, the buildings of Jaipur exemplify its decline. Even in the earliest of them, the traditional architectural details lack vigour and depth; they are flattened so that they become relief sculpture on the building's surface, and sometimes they are simply drawn on in white outline. In an architecture where the details are merely drawn, they are evidently not taken very seriously, and in time the architects of Jaipur found that it is as easy to draw classical as Indian forms: from the mid-nineteenth century, round columns and fanlights began to appear on the domestic buildings of the city's streets (fig. 9).

Further west, in the Rajasthan desert, the architects of Jaisalmer had adhered to traditional standards with more determination. In the eighteenth century, they had further refined a long-established practice of stone-carving, and they richly embellished the exteriors of palaces and *havelis* (courtyard houses). These buildings are therefore among the few exceptions to the general decline of Rajput architecture, for although the old forms are (as elsewhere) made small and multiplied in number, they are still crisply and deeply carved. The excellence of the carving was sustained into the nineteenth century, for the finest examples include the famous Patua ki Haveli (c. 1805) and Salim Singh ki Haveli (c. 1815) and even the rather later Badal Vilas – a palace built by Maharawal Bairi Sal (r. 1864-91). Before the end of the century, however, the European influence had reached the western desert. It first appeared in the house of a state minister or *diwan*, Nathmal ki Haveli (c. 1885). Inserted into the usual elaborate stone-carving on the facade is a little sculpture of a train, and another of a horse and carriage. This suggests that, at an early stage, the fascination was less with European architecture than with European invention; but architectural forms soon followed: the gate added as an entrance to the Gadisar tank on the south-eastern edge of the city (and known as Tilon ki Pol after the patroness, whom a local guide described as 'a religious-minded prostitute'[37]) is equipped with a classical balustrade along its roof. In the palaces built at the turn of the century by Bairi Sal's successor, Maharawal Jawahar Singh, the European influence is more pronounced. The Jawahar Vilas (fig. 10) has feeble classical pediments and inexact Corinthian capitals on strange, fluted columns (with Mughal bases), and an inner court is decorated with mass-produced tiles. The slightly later Jawahar Niwas, outside the city, takes a decisive step further, for it is classical in its proportions, and it is devoid of the usual intricate stone-carving. The rooms and their details are executed on a generous European scale rather than the traditional Indian small scale; and features such as balconies – which earlier had been made small and elaborately decorated – have here been inflated, made dull and heavy, and stuck to the facades of a classically regular block.

Another part of Rajasthan which shows a remarkably late survival of a local tradition is Shekhavati. Lying to the north of Jaipur, this district contains a number of small towns, such as Nawalgarh, Fatehpur, Mandawa and Sikar, each of

which is a congregation of vast *havelis*, now mostly empty and crumbling. These *havelis* were built by the rich merchants of the district, the Marwaris.[38] The merchants had not made their fortunes in their quiet home towns: they had been responsible for the servicing of the Mughal Empire, and with its decline, they serviced instead the British Empire and travelled to Calcutta and Bombay to attend the new masters. Much of their earnings, however, they sent home to the district of their birth. Religious tradition enjoined them to undertake a number of building projects for the public good: each was expected to provide a temple, a school, a well, a *dharamsala* (pilgrims' lodge) and a *gausala* (cow shed). But each merchant would have wished in addition to build an impressive *haveli* to serve as a home base and to house those members of his family who did not accompany him on his quest for wealth. Naturally enough, the Shekhavati *havelis* vie with each other in size, fashionableness and splendour.

Most of the surviving *havelis* were built in the nineteenth or early twentieth centuries. Their architectural style is that of the region – they are related to the Rajput maharajas' palaces, such as those at Jodhpur and Jaipur – and like the *havelis* of Jaisalmer, they sustained local tradition for a surprisingly long time. They remain, for example, entirely traditional in planning, with small apartments arranged around two *chowks* (courtyards), an outer one where visitors were received and business conducted, and an inner one for private family use.

10. Jaisalmer; Jawahar Vilas (1890s).

21

The planning of individual rooms is similarly traditional: small spaces of complicated form are further subdivided and complicated by arcades and by changes in the level of the floor. European influence is not pervasive; it consists, as elsewhere, of the occasional interpolation of classical columns and shuttered windows with fanlights into an otherwise undisturbed traditional scheme (fig. 12). In the Gauri Lal Biyani Haveli in Sikar, built early in this century, the ceilings are supported by steel joists, but this potentially transforming new technology did not encourage the architects to depart from established planning patterns (to the evident inconvenience of the present inappropriate tenant, the local electricity board). Some *havelis* are entirely free of European features, though the interpolations became commoner towards the end of the nineteenth century. Some of the later *havelis* in Fatehpur have deep verandas across their facades, like those of colonial bungalows.

The Shekhavati *havelis* are famous for their painted walls; for the Marwaris, perhaps in an attempt to compensate for the colourless landscape of northern Rajasthan, had their houses covered, inside and out, with bold and vivid murals. Complementing the architecture, the murals generally are related to Rajput palace decoration and show a long continuation of traditional subject-matter, style and technique. The most popular subjects are scenes from the Hindu scriptures, especially events in the lives of Krishna, Hanuman and Laxmi; secular themes include Rajas, horsemen, and scenes from Rajasthani folk tales such as the story of Dhola and Maru; corners are filled up with flower patterns. All are treated in strong, flat colours. The first mark of European influence in the murals is the appearance of a new range of subjects: Krishna is upstaged by ladies and gentlemen in Western dress, and the subjects that lent themselves to long compositions – like the army pursuing Dhola and Maru – give way to steam trains (fig. 11).[39] Later, the style too was affected, as attempts were made at those pictorial devices that are most developed in Western art, devices such as perspective, modelling and subtle colouring. It cannot be said that these attempts were successful or enhanced the visual power of the murals. The artists abandoned established practices to grapple with unfamiliar techniques which they mastered only crudely. While the older paintings are among the finest examples of mural art in India, and the first depictions of trains have an amusing naïvety, the late, Westernized paintings are vulgar and incompetent.

Bikaner, in the northern corner of Rajasthan, is almost as inaccessible as Jaisalmer in the west, and again the vogue for classical insertions took some time in coming. The principal palace of the maharajas is typical of many Rajput palaces in being contained within a substantial fort and consisting of a congeries of apartments built over an extended period, with parts added by each successive ruler. The additions made by Maharaja Dungar Singh (r. 1872-87) include a tower, which is conventionally Indian in design except for a classical arcade sketched across its facade in low relief. The unusual degree of inaccuracy in the details – for the capitals are of no known order and the entablature is of Indian

11. Nawalgarh,
Shekhavati district;
*Choo choo gari* (late
nineteenth-century
*haveli* mural).

12. Nawalgarh,
Shekhavati district;
detail of part of the Aath
Haveli group (late
nineteenth century).

13. Bikaner; decoration in the Chatra Mahal, Junagadh Palace (c. 1880).

14. Bikaner; Ganga Niwas Chowk, Junagadh Palace (1887-96).

flamboyance – reflects Bikaner's remoteness from major centres of British building activity. At the top of the palace, Dungar Singh added a pavilion known as the Chatra Mahal, strategically placed to catch the few breezes passing through his desert kingdom. Traditionally in a Rajput palace, the interior walls of such an important pavilion would receive special attention; they would be covered with mirror-work, inlaid coloured glass or murals. Here, they are covered in English china: an impressive collection of tiles and strainers adorns every surface (fig. 13). In a period of stylistic stagnation, the appeal of a novelty drove out traditional techniques. As a cultural influence, this china is analogous to Shah Jahan's Italian *pietra dura* panels, though the Maharaja's taste is less commendable than the Emperor's.

The most substantial additions to the Bikaner palace were made by Dungar Singh's successor, Maharaja Sir Ganga Singh (r. 1887-1943). These include the courtyard known as Ganga Niwas Chowk, built at the beginning of his reign (fig. 14). Here, Indian and inexact European forms divide the storeys between them: above are *jarokhas* (cradle balconies) enclosed with *jalis* (perforated

24

screens) and capped by drooping *bangaldar* eaves; below, imperfectly round arches are supported on columns with faintly Corinthian capitals and fluted bases. The courtyard gives access to a vast *darbar* hall, built at the same time. Coming from the courtyard, one is surprised to find this hall entirely Indian in detail. Its dimensions (and the engineering that facilitated them) are European, but nothing else is: there are no interpolations. All over their considerable surface, the walls are carved with Indian motifs, producing an effect like a giant Kashmir casket. In making use of European technology while retaining exclusively indigenous architectural details, the architects satisfied the express wish of the Maharaja[40] and at last came to terms with European influence. But if this hall demonstrates a more considered approach and a more resolved style, it is an example of a rare phenomenon.

# CHAPTER TWO

# Pax Britannica
# and the New Breed

With the rise in the power of the East India Company in the early nineteenth century, the maharajas who ruled independent states within India established treaties with the Company, and by doing so ensured the perpetuation of their rule throughout the remaining period of the British presence. These independent or Native States accounted for over two-fifths of India's land mass, so that British India was never the whole of India, and indeed until Independence the term 'India' described a geographical region, not a nation. The treaties established 'perpetual friendship' between the states and the British; each maharaja was required to acknowledge the 'supremacy' of the British Government, but was assured that 'the Maharaja and his heirs and successors shall be absolute rulers of their country, and the British jurisdiction shall not be introduced into that principality.'[1] The return for the recognition of supremacy was that the British undertook to 'protect the principality and territory' of each state, to rescue it from any external aggression; but the corollary of this was that the maharaja was forbidden to initiate aggression with any other state.[2] The maharaja not only became a friend of the British, he was obliged to become a friend of his neighbours. By this means, the British sought to impose peace on the warring Indian rulers; the attempt was not instantly successful but the treaties endured – with the transfer of power from the Company to the Crown after 1857, they were renewed in similar terms – and in time peace was guaranteed. The maharajas were effectively debarred from what had hitherto been their usual and preferred occupation.

The reduction in warfare saved the maharajas not only energy but considerable amounts of money, and both could now be spent on another long-favoured pastime: building. Traditional Indian palaces are fortified, but the treaties had obviated the need for defences, so many maharajas began to build a new kind of palace: not hilltop retreats but mansions on the plains. The treaties also brought the maharajas more into contact with Britons, and gave rise to occasions when they had to entertain the new overlords. In the nineteenth century, few Britons were adventurous enough to want entertainment in the Indian fashion, and some maharajas were happy to provide ballrooms and billiard rooms instead. The small, cramped apartments of traditional palaces where one sat on a floor strewn with quilts and velvet bolsters were abandoned in favour of spacious halls where one could sit on European furniture. Apart from satisfying guests, these new amenities also suited the increasingly Westernized tastes of the maharajas themselves.

So while in some parts of India, a European influence was reflected in the introduction into the architecture of some classical details, in other parts there was a much more fundamental influence, as the rulers wanted an altogether new kind of palace. Often, the new palaces were wholly classical in style; and to be sure that the details would be correct, a maharaja employed not the native craftsmen of his own state but an English architect. Examples of classical palaces built for maharajas may be found throughout the subcontinent: in the north, the Maharaja of Kashmir built a Grecian palace at Srinagar, and the Sikh Maharajas of Kapurthala commissioned both the Italianate Villa Buona Vista and the French Beaux-Arts Elysée Palace; the far east of the subcontinent had its own Italian Renaissance in the palaces of Cooch Behar and Tripura; in the south, the Nizam of Hyderabad spent a fragment of his legendary wealth on the extensive, classical Falaknuma Palace; on the western seaboard, in the palaces of Porbandar and Morvi, the classicism was (perhaps not entirely inappropriately) somewhat Venetian in inspiration; and, in the centre, vast classical palaces arose at Panna and Indore. And these are only a few of the many classical palaces that were built in the Native States between the mid-nineteenth and the early twentieth centuries.

One of the most ambitious was the Jai Vilas at Gwalior, commissioned by Maharaja Jayaji Rao Scindia (r. 1843-86) and completed in 1874 to designs by Lt. Col. Sir Michael Filose (fig. 15). One of the largest palaces in India, it is an exercise in superlatives. It contains, for example, the largest chandeliers in the world, each of which is forty-two feet high, weighs three tons and carries two hundred and forty-eight candles.[3] Its first guest was the most eminent attainable, the Prince of Wales. Nor was it to be outdone in gimmickry: in the dining room stood an electrically-illuminated rock garden, and the port was passed by a miniature silver train which ran along the top of the table.

The vogue for interpolating classical motifs in Indian buildings was accounted for above as an attempt to reinvigorate a flagging indigenous tradition. The more radical process, the building of wholly classical palaces, occurred chiefly in regions that were governed by rulers who had little in the way of cultural traditions at all, flagging or otherwise. The Rajput maharajas of Rajasthan had long pedigrees, going back in some cases to the seventh century, and their court culture was highly developed even if it was in decline; this explains why the European influence was comparatively limited in Rajasthan, for though the Rajput maharajas adopted some aspects of European civilization – notably its furniture, pictures and ornaments – these were adopted as decorative

15. Gwalior; Jai Vilas,
by Sir Michael Filose
(1874).

16. Indore; interior of
Lalbagh Palace, built for
Maharaja Sivaji Rao
Holkar (1880s).

28

clutter, and the examples of entirely Western-style buildings constructed by the Rajputs are few in number and late in date. The Maratha maharajas, by contrast, were a new breed of ruler. Until relatively recent times, the Marathas had been passive peasants; it was the turmoil of the decline of the Mughal Empire which turned them into a martial people and threw up vigorous leaders among them. These new leaders had no lineage, no inherited court culture, and so they were readier to adopt the civilization of the people who became their imperial overlords. The Scindias of Gwalior were among the most dominant of the Maratha ruling families. Their Maratha neighbours and rivals, the Holkars, were swift to follow the example set at Gwalior: in the 1880s, they built their own great classical palace at their capital, Indore (fig. 16).

It was not only, however, their lack of a cultural inheritance which led these maharajas to adopt the architectural style of the imperial overlord; they were responding to a range of forces. In addition to the process of passive Westernization – by which Indians voluntarily copied fashions that historical chance presented to their view – these forces included the deliberate policy of active Westernization on the part of the British Government.

### The Policy of Westernization

In the early years of Company rule, the British had consciously adopted the mantle of the Mughals; they became, to an extent, Oriental rulers. They followed, for example, the traditional pattern in the patronage of learning: Warren Hastings founded a college of Arabic and Persian Studies in Calcutta, and Jonathan Duncan (an assistant to Cornwallis) founded a Sanskrit College in Benares. With the sounder establishment of their power in the early nineteenth century, reflected in the treaties with the maharajas, the British perceived for themselves a new and more responsible role. They began to see it as their duty to rebuild and govern a country which had been devastated by continual internal feuding since the death of the Mughal Emperor Aurangzeb in 1707. For such a task, new policies were needed.

In the debate about how India should be ruled, the principal protagonists included Evangelicals such as William Wilberforce, who were appalled by certain Indian social customs and felt a Christian duty to intervene in what they considered a pagan and therefore damned society. A similar duty was felt by Utilitarians such as James Mill, though their zeal was not Christian but rationalist: entirely confident of the superiority of the Western world, they believed it to be a society based on reason rather than superstition, and they wished to share the benefit with all mankind. The Evangelicals and Utilitarians were able to argue their case for intervention entirely undistracted by actual acquaintance with India. Opposing them were conservatives, many of whom, like Warren Hastings himself, were well apprised of the practical complexities that attended alien rule in India. The conservatives argued that Indian society should be left alone, that it was enough to provide a framework of security for trade. Some who were serving in India at the time – such as Charles Metcalfe, the Governor of Delhi – urged caution. Change, even where desirable, must be gradual, they insisted, so as to respect Indian sensibilities and institutions.

It was the interventionists who won the debate, however, and they established certain principles which underlay British rule in India for the remainder of its course. Their victory was achieved partly fortuitously, through the appointment of Lord William Bentinck as Governor-General from 1828 to 1835. Bentinck, who secured the post partly through family influence and partly because of his reputation as a disciplinarian, happened also to be a Benthamite and a humanist, with no sympathy for Indian civilization. He swiftly initiated policies of social reform. Some of these, and notably the suppression of *sati* (widow burning) and of *thuggee* (ritual robbery and murder), were relatively uncontroversial, as many Indians welcomed them. More contentious were his policies regarding education. Even before Bentinck arrived in India, a dispute had arisen between those who advocated the Westernization of Indian learning and those who wished to continue support for Oriental traditions. The most eloquent spokesmen among the latter group were English scholars of Indian literature and religion, such as Sir William Jones, who insisted on their merits. But Bentinck clearly sided with the Westernizers. Indian support here was rather more limited, though Bentinck did find an ally in the Bengali leader Ram Mohan Roy, who showed how much had changed since the days of Hastings by helping to establish a college for the propagation of Western learning.

Bentinck acquired another formidable ally in 1834. The recent India Bill provided for a new, non-Company member of the Supreme Council of India, and the first man to hold this post was Thomas Babington Macaulay. The new member displayed an interest in the education debate and was appointed to adjudicate in it, with the result that a resolution was passed in March 1835 declaring that 'the great object of the British Government ought to be the promotion of European literature and science among the natives of India.'[4] Macaulay was immediately involved in putting this policy into effect through the founding of schools which employed English as the medium of instruction.

The policy had an inestimable impact on the development of civilization in India – an impact still being felt – and so it is worth looking closer at its origin and at the man who was chiefly responsible. Macaulay took the post on the Supreme Council not through any desire to visit India; indeed, he regarded his time there as an 'exile'.[5] In taking it, he was sensible equally of the crucial responsibility he would hold, and of the salary of ten thousand pounds per annum.[6] On the journey out, by his own account, he was very unsociable: he spent the time in his cabin reading works in Greek, Latin, Spanish, Italian, French and English. He prepared himself for India by reading James Mill's *History of British India* (1817), the work of a man who had never visited the country. Macaulay spent three and a half years in India, during which his read-

ing continued to centre on the classics. His letters to his friend Thomas Flower
Ellis, are full of comment and disputation on the classics;[7] at the end of 1835, he
recalled the reading he had done since unpacking his books in Calcutta:

> During the last thirteen months I have read Aeschylus twice; Sophocles
> twice; Euripedes once; Pindar twice; Callimachus; Apollonious Rhodius;
> Quintus Calaber; Theocritus twice; Herodotus; Thucydides; almost all
> Xenophon's works; almost all Plato; Aristotle's Politics, and a good deal
> of his Organon, besides dipping elsewhere in him; the whole of Plutarch's
> Lives; about half of Lucian; two or three books of Athenaeus; Plautus
> twice; Terence twice; Lucretius twice; Catullus; Tibullus; Propertius;
> Lucan; Statius; Silius Italicus; Livy; Velleius Paterculus; Sallust; Caesar;
> and, lastly, Cicero. I have, indeed, still a little of Cicero left; but I shall
> finish him in a few days. I am now deep in Aristophanes and Lucian.[8]

While admiring this astounding appetite, one might wonder whether he could
not have found reading-matter more closely relevant to his occupation in India.
Macaulay was stunningly adept at learning languages – a skill he displayed while
in India by learning Portuguese in order to read Camoens's *Lusiad*[9] – but his
attempts to master the complexities of Sanskrit and Persian were short-lived.
He claimed to have read translations of 'the most celebrated Arabic and Sanscrit
works',[10] but there is no sign that he studied them with the attention that he be-
stowed on the classics: there are no boastful menus of Hindu epics, of Persian
histories, or of any of the other works that might have revealed to him the main-
springs of Indian society.[11] Residence in India did not revise Macaulay's complete lack of interest in, even contempt for, civilizations not derived from Greek
or Roman antiquity. His letters contain few observations of Indian people, landscape or architecture. In a letter to Ellis of 1834, he attempted to persuade his
friend to abandon the study of exotic peoples and translate Herodotus instead: 'I
would not give the worst page in Clarendon or Fra Paolo for all that ever was, or
ever will be, written about the migrations of the Leleges and the laws of the
Oscans.'[12]

The depth of Macaulay's ignorance of Indian attitudes is revealed by his
assumption about the long-term effects of his English-medium schools:

> No Hindoo, who has received an English education, ever remains
> sincerely attached to his religion. Some continue to profess it as a matter
> of policy; but many profess themselves pure Deists, and some embrace
> Christianity. It is my firm belief that, if our plans of education are
> followed up, there will not be a single idolater among the respectable
> classes in Bengal thirty years hence. . . . I heartily rejoice in the prospect.[13]

Had he observed more, he would have known that Hinduism is tenacious, that
the Hindu adheres to his religion when he has given up everything else. Not just
thirty, but one hundred and fifty years on, despite the continuance of English-

medium education among the wealthier classes even after Independence, these Westernized classes still contain any number of respectable idolaters, while Christianity has remained most widespread among the poorer and poorly educated sections of the population (who espouse it often only because it offers, or is expected to offer, an escape from Hindu caste prejudice).

Macaulay's incautious prophecy was made in a letter to his father. In his official writings, he did not cite conversions to Christianity as a desired consequence of English education. Publicly, he adhered to the Government policy of neutrality on religious issues, though not without a certain duplicity. Responding to one of the arguments of the Orientalists, he noted that

> It is said that the Sanscrit and Arabic are the languages in which the sacred books of a hundred millions of people are written, and that they are, on that account, entitled to peculiar encouragement. Assuredly it is the duty of the British Government in India to be not only tolerant, but neutral on all religious questions. But to encourage the study of a literature admitted to be of small intrinsic value, only because that literature inculcates the most serious errors on the most important subjects, is a course hardly reconcilable with reason, with morality, or even with that neutrality which ought, as we all agree, to be sacredly preserved.[14]

How, then, does this passage stand the tests of reason, morality and neutrality? The assertion that Eastern religions contain 'the most serious errors on the most important subjects' must be admitted – even by those who believe it to be true – to be scarcely an expression of neutrality. And it was dishonest of Macaulay to pretend that introducing the study of English in place of Sanskrit and Arabic would not have an actively detrimental effect on India's religions: it was bound to have (indeed, now has had) the effect of severing the educated Indian from the texts that expound his religion, so that, while he may adhere to the religion itself, his knowledge of it is often somewhat inexact.

In logic, in rhetoric and in attitude, this passage is typical of the document of which it forms a part, Macaulay's famous 'Minute on Education'.[15] This minute was written for the benefit of the Committee on Public Instruction, of which Macaulay was the President and whose other members were divided equally between Orientalists and Westernizers. Macaulay insisted on the value of English as a medium: 'Whoever knows that language has ready access to all the vast intellectual wealth which all the wisest nations of the earth have created and hoarded in the course of the ninety generations'.[16] He argued that English was already widely known throughout the world, and was likely to become the major language of commerce. In this, of course, he has been proved correct, though his remarks were, to a degree, a self-fulfilling prophecy: English became a major language of commerce partly as a result of the imperial policies based on his minute.

Macaulay's claims for the value of the English language and of Western learning are coupled, in the minute, with a display of contempt for Indian civilization:

> The question now before us is simply whether, when it is in our power to teach this language, we shall teach languages in which, by universal confession, there are no books on any subject which deserve to be compared to our own; whether, when we can teach European science, we shall teach systems which, by universal confession, whenever they differ from those of Europe, differ for the worse, and whether, when we can patronise sound Philosophy and true History we shall countenance, at the public expense, medical doctrines, which would disgrace an English farrier; Astronomy, which would move laughter in the girls at an English boarding-school; History, abounding with kings thirty feet high, and reigns thirty thousand years long; and Geography, made up of seas of treacle and seas of butter.[17]

It is a mark of fine rhetoric but also of inferior reason that he could describe a vulgar prejudice as 'universal confession': the dissent of half of his committee ought to have persuaded him that such views were not universal among those who were well acquainted with Indian literature. His caricature of Indian history, as it is recounted in Hindu religious texts, would be no less applicable to the Bible, and recently a spirited defence has even been made for Indian medieval science.[18]

Macaulay's inclusion in the minute of expressions of contempt for Indian civilization was no gratuitous self-indulgence: that contempt was an integral part of the policy. Westernization did not mean simply offering Indians the advantages of Western civilization, it meant substituting that civilization for local traditions. Macaulay's declared aim was to raise 'a class of persons, Indian in blood and colour, but English in taste, in opinions, in morals and in intellect'.[19] It was not a matter of addition: for an Indian, being Westernized entailed disowning his own heritage as well as espousing a new one.

In his total confidence in the superiority of Western civilization and his contempt for the East, Macaulay was echoing others of his time; but also, because he was an eloquent and powerful exponent of these attitudes, he helped to propagate them, and so helped to shape British perceptions of Indian civilization in the mid-nineteenth century. Since those more widely shared perceptions themselves became potent, and helped to shape even Indian attitudes towards Indian civilization, they should be briefly surveyed.

*Indian Architecture and the British*

British attitudes to Indian architecture have not been constant. The first accurate and readily accessible information about it was provided by the aquatint views published in 1785-88 by William Hodges in his *Select Views of India*, and by those published by the Daniells in the six volumes of their *Oriental Scenery* between

1795 and 1808. Of course, opinions about Indian architecture had been expressed long before any such accurate information was available, but the present survey may ignore those early opinions, as they are largely fantastic and exerted no influence in India. The volumes of Hodges and the Daniells were popular among English audiences, gratifying the Georgian taste for the exotic. They partly inspired and became the manuals for the Georgian Indian style, itself a further reflection of increasing British interest in Indian forms. While remodelling the Guildhall in 1788, George Dance referred to the plates of Hodges, as did Samuel Pepys Cockerell while remodelling Daylesford (the home of Hodges's patron Warren Hastings) in 1793, though the Indian features of both buildings are unobtrusive. Progressing from these tentative beginnings, the same Cockerell engaged Thomas Daniell (then widely recognized as the leading authority on Indian architecture) to assist him in the remodelling of the house and garden of Sezincote for his nabob brother between 1805 and 1811 (fig. 17). While this was going on, William Porden added a vast, ostensibly Mughal stable to the Royal Pavilion at Brighton, and a little later the pavilion itself was remodelled by John Nash.

Meanwhile in India, rising British interest in Indian monuments was reflected in the pictures of them commissioned from Indian artists. After the British capture of Delhi and Agra in 1803, the great Mughal monuments became more accessible to Western eyes, and many who visited them demanded pictures as souvenirs; they found able and willing suppliers among the Indian draughtsmen who had been initiated into the techniques of perspective drawing in the offices of British engineers.

This early period of interest corresponds to the period before the policy changes of the Bentinck era, which were accompanied by a dramatic change in attitude to the Indian cultural heritage in general and to its architecture in particular. In Bentick's time, there was much wanton destruction of buildings, motivated not by any iconoclastic zeal but simply by the pursuit of practical convenience. Consider the testimony of General Sir William Sleeman. This officer was in some ways a typical Bentinck man – he was, for example, the Governor-General's principal agent in the suppression of *thuggee* – but for many aspects of Indian life, he retained an old-fashioned respect, and his memoirs reveal a considerable receptivity towards Indian people and things. Of the Mughal Red Fort in Agra, he wrote:

> The Marquis of Hastings, when Governor-General of India, broke up one of the most beautiful of the marble baths of this palace to send home to George IV of England, then Prince Regent; and the rest of the marble of the suite of apartments from which it had been taken, with all its exquisite fret-work and mosaic, was afterwards sold by auction, on account of our government, by order of the then Governor-General, Lord W. Bentinck. Had these things fetched the price expected, it is probable that the whole

of the palace, and even the Taj itself, would have been pulled down, and sold in the same manner.[20]

This account records a significant change in attitude: the earlier act of dismantling the bath could be said to have reflected an interest in the Indian building, even if not a respect for its integrity, for it was assumed that the Prince Regent would enjoy the piece (though, in fact, he never received it); but the later destruction and auction was simple vandalism and opportunism. Bentinck's order suggests an underlying attitude to Indian architecture which is the counterpart to Macaulay's attitude to Indian literature. Such acts of unconcerned destruction became common and led the high Victorian Fergusson to deplore 'the ruthless barbarism of our rule'.[21]

Nothing strengthened the hold of Macaulayite views in India so much as the episode known as the Sepoy Mutiny of 1857. This is somewhat ironic, since the mutiny was in part a display of resentment against the too rapid pace of Macaulayite Westernization: certainly, the immediate sparking issues, such as the episode of the greased cartridges, involved Indian perceptions that their traditions were being trampled on. But far from arresting the policy of Westernization, the

17. Sezincote, Gloucestershire; remodelled by S.P. Cockerell and Thomas Daniell (1805-11).

mutiny persuaded Britons of the intrinsic horror of India and enhanced their resolve to change it. Their contempt for Indian art was strengthened, too. That arbiter of mid-Victorian taste, John Ruskin, detested Indian art and architecture as the products of an idolatrous people. Like many, he considered that 1857 had revealed Indians to be cruel and treacherous, and he argued – in a typical application of the art historian's pathetic fallacy – that one must expect the art of an immoral society to be bad.

Ruskin's most considered remarks on Indian art come in *The Two Paths*, a series of lectures given in the year following the mutiny. Early in the first lecture, he reflected on that episode:

> Since the race of man began its course of sin on this earth, nothing has been done by it so significant of all bestial, and lower than bestial, degradation, as the acts of the Indian race in the year that has just passed by. Cruelty as fierce may indeed have been wreaked, and brutality as abominable been practised before, but never under like circumstances . . . cruelty stretched to its fiercest against the gentle and unoffending, and corruption festered to its loathsomest in the midst of the witnessing presence of a disciplined civilization, – these we could not have known to be within the practicable compass of human guilt, but for the acts of the Indian mutineer.[22]

The mutiny presented Ruskin with a dilemma. He had been visiting Scotland and found that country to be full of virtuous people but devoid of art; and the comparison with India – which had been shown to be full of wicked people but which, one had to concede, was productive of much highly refined art – pointed him towards the unattractive conclusion that art is the product of cruel minds. Triumphantly, though, he sighted a solution to the dilemma:

> It is quite true that the art of India is delicate and refined. But it has one curious character distinguishing it from all other art of equal merit in design – *it never represents a natural fact*. . . . To all the facts and forms of nature it wilfully and resolutely opposes itself: it will not draw a man, but an eight-armed monster; it will not draw a flower, but only a spiral or a zigzag. It thus indicates that the people who practise it are cut off from all possible sources of healthy knowledge or natural delight. . . . They lie bound in the dungeon of their own corruption.[23]

In short, Indian art could be seen as unnatural, the characteristic expression of an unnatural people.[24]

In the aftermath of the mutiny, the British authorities contemplated destroying the Mughal Red Fort in Delhi, as an act of vengeance against the citizens of a major centre of the uprising. Insensitive, now, to its architectural beauties, what an earlier generation had visited as tourists and bought pictures of, they saw only as a political symbol. Some Englishmen urged its complete destruction and replacement by a Fort Victoria; others wanted the city's principal, seventeenth-century mosque to be replaced by a cathedral.[25] Neither happened, though within the fort many palace apartments were swept away by the military, in order to make space for what the artist Val Prinsep later called 'a kind of howling desert of barracks, hideous, British and pretentious.'[26] At the same time in Agra, the railway station was built so close to the city's main mosque as to destroy half its entrance and all its peacefulness. This careless indifference to the architectural heritage was the keynote of the attitude of the British Government in India for much of the nineteenth century.

At home, too, interest was declining. The mutiny made India briefly topical, but generally also less admired. It has been argued by Patrick Connor that Indian design, already associated with the extravagance of George IV, now became associated as well with the atrocities of 1857 and fell sharply out of fashion.[27]

But there was a further change in the latter part of the century, with a second tide of enthusiasm for the country's architecture. This development depended upon scholarship, and the principle figure in this context was James Fergusson. With the publication of his *History of Indian and Eastern Architecture* in 1876, Fergusson began the systematic study of Indian architectural history. In 1862, General Sir Alexander Cunningham had founded the Archaeological Survey of India, with the intention of cataloguing the country's ancient monuments. The Survey became a department of the Government, but it was not initially taken very seriously, in spite of the quality of the work done by Cunningham and some of his assistants, including James Burgess. Its aim, as its name implies, was simply to survey, not to conserve; it was therefore seen as a temporary institution, and after the retirement of Cunningham in 1885 its work was severely restricted. However, at the turn of the century, during the viceroyalty of Curzon, it was revived under the directorship of J.H. Marshall; it was given a new brief to conserve as well as to record, and it began a lavish programme of publications.

The renewed examination of Indian buildings led to a renewed vogue for Indian forms in buildings at home. In 1884, the Duke and Duchess of Connaught commissioned an Indian-style billiard room for Bagshot Park.[28] In 1890, the Queen gave expression to her new role as India's Empress by commissioning a dining room in the Indian style for Osborne, on the Isle of Wight. Both rooms were designed by John Lockwood Kipling, the latter with the help of the Punjabi craftsman Ram Singh. Three years later, Lord Iveagh added an Indian hall to Elveden in Suffolk (a house which had formerly belonged to the deposed maharaja of the Punjab, Duleep Singh).

The third and most remarkable component of the new enthusiasm, however, was the development in the last quarter of the century of a new style for imperial architecture in India. The hegemony of the classical had already been broken by a rise in the popularity of the Gothic, but now British architects in India began to examine the Indian tradition and to attempt to adapt Indian styles to British imperial buildings. These experiments in what has generally been called Indo-Saracenic architecture, include Islamic-style railway termini and university colleges (which are discussed further below).

The late nineteenth-century revival of interest in Indian architecture was much more substantial and serious than the eighteenth-century movement had been, and it contained the roots of modern scholarship on the subject. But it did not eradicate established antipathies. The work of Fergusson, Cunningham and Burgess increased awareness and stopped the unconcerned destruction of Indian monuments; but though fewer among the British public in India and at home still dismissed Indian civilization summarily as Macaulay had done, they were not all converted to a sympathy for it. The late eighteenth-century sympathizers such as Hodges had been confronting nothing worse than ignorance; the new generation of enthusiasts were confronting prejudice, and they could no longer interest an audience in Indian architecture simply by showing it. Writing on Indian art and architecture – even by some who professed an enthusiasm – continued to reflect a Christian unease, especially with the more mystical aspects of Hindu iconography. Thus, Sir George Birdwood, a leading champion of India's industrial arts and crafts, felt less comfortable with the sculpture that adorns the country's temples, declaring that 'the monstrous shapes of the Puranic deities are unsuitable for the higher forms of artistic representation; and this is possibly why sculpture and painting are unknown, as fine arts, in India.' Birdwood's remarks were echoed early in this century by Vincent Smith:

> After AD 300 Indian sculpture properly so called hardly deserves to be reckoned as art. The figures both of men and animals become stiff and formal, perception of the facts of nature almost disappears, and the idea of power is clumsily expressed by the multiplication of members. The many-headed, many-armed gods and goddesses whose images crowd the walls and roofs of medieval temples have no pretensions to beauty and are frequently hideous and grotesque.[29]

Comment of this sort was so persistent that A.K. Coomaraswamy (the first great art historian from the subcontinent itself) devoted an article to calling for 'criticism a little more penetrating than is involved in merely counting heads and arms'.[30] Coomaraswamy perceived that the objection made by Birdwood and Smith proceeded from an antipathy to the thing expressed as much as to the manner of expression, and he complained that it was scarcely fair to fault a Hindu sculptor for illustrating Hindu themes as they are described in scripture. Putting it differently, one might say that the objection entails a refusal to accept that Indian art has its own distinct aims and conventions; Birdwood and Smith denied that Indian sculpture was fine art because it offends against Western conceptions of beauty. In short, they were no cultural pluralists, but measured all art by their own canon.

Their complaints about unnatural gods echo those of Ruskin already quoted, not only in language but also in logic. Ruskin's notion that the basis of great art lies in the imitation of nature, was derived from the classical canon; and so when he directly compared Hindu and Greek depictions of a bull and derided the Hindu rendering for being less naturalistic,[31] he might just as well have derided it for being less Greek. This Procrustean approach has been a common habit in British appreciation of Eastern art, in spite of the entreaties of a percipient few who have seen that not all art pursues the same ideals. Among those ignored few was the first serious apologist for Indian architecture, William Hodges:

> That great Grecian Architecture comprizes all that is excellent in the art, I cannot help considering as a doctrine, which is in itself as erroneous and servile, as in its consequences it is destructive of every hope of improvement . . . why should we admire it in an exclusive manner; or, blind to the majesty, boldness, and magnificence of the Egyptian, Hindoo, Moorish, and Gothic, as admirable wonders of architecture, unmercifully blame and despise them, because they are more various in their forms, and not reducible to the precise rules of the Greek hut . . .?[32]

A century earlier, the French traveller François Bernier stumbled on a similar perception: finding that he admired the Taj Mahal, he realized with some disquiet that he must have 'imbibed an Indian taste'.[33] And two centuries after Bernier, Lady Sleeman visited the same building with her husband, who interrupted his musings on the tomb's narrow escape from destruction at the hands of Bentinck, to ask his wife what she thought of it: '"I cannot", said she, "tell you what I think, for I know not how to criticise such a building, but I can tell you what I feel. I would die tomorrow to have such another over me!"'[34]

To those less ready than Bernier or Lady Sleeman to acknowledge the existence of a distinctly Indian taste, and of non-Western criteria of criticism – to those who remained adamant that Western values alone hold the touchstone of artistic excellence – buildings such as the Taj Mahal presented a problem, for in spite of being Indian, they are undeniably great architecture. One way around this problem was to claim that the Taj Mahal and any other indisputably fine Indian buildings were in reality Western buildings in disguise: it was asserted that they were built by Europeans or under their influence. Hence there is a long tradition of attributing the design of the Taj Mahal to Italian jewellers.[35] The technique was in use as early as 1590, when Gasparo Balbi was so impressed by the Hindu rock-cut temple at Elephanta that he attributed it to Alexander the Great.[36] For those who indulged in it, the reattribution of Indian architectural masterpieces was doubly satisfying, for it both claimed for Western civilization a stake in the splendours of the East, and delivered a back-handed insult to the Indian tradition which was shown to be incapable of producing anything fine without assistance. It confirmed what many had always suspected of Indian architecture: that it was basically no good.

## Indian Reactions

The British Government's policy of Westernizing Indian society, and expressions of contempt for Indian civilization made by members of the ruling race, both encouraged in the educated Indian a scepticism about his own cultural heritage. As J.L. Maffey observed in 1903, 'it is impossible for a native of India to imbibe English education without losing his admiration for the indigenous arts of his country'.[37] The same forces encouraged him instead to espouse Western standards of civilization: to want to build, for example, in classical styles.

That choice was further encouraged by the clear identification of classicism as a style of power. Since the new impetus which British building in India had received around 1800, buildings had been intimately associated with British power. Sometimes, indeed, they were its substitute: the new Government Houses and Residencies constructed then were deliberately ostentatious; they made a show of splendour to suggest power, in the hope that the appearance of power would be as effective, while being cheaper than acquisition of the reality. In defence of Wellesley's extravagance at Calcutta, Lord Valentia remarked famously: 'India is a country of splendour . . . the Head of a mighty Empire ought to conform himself to the prejudices of the country he rules over. . . . In short, I wish India to be ruled from a palace, not from a counting-house. . . .'[38] And if buildings were power, they were also classical. Until about 1850, the palace was always classical, so that classicism gathered to itself all the prestige and authority of British rule.

By building a classical palace, therefore, an Indian maharaja made a bid for comparable authority, whereas by continuing to patronize Indian styles, he would be associating himself with something condemned by that same authority as worthless. The Government House in Calcutta was scarcely complete before the Nawab of Bengal began to commission plans for an imitation of it for his own use, to be built at Murshidabad.[39]

The feeling that a social or political prestige ensued from a cultural alignment with the British cannot, perhaps, be documented from writings by the maharajas themselves. Until modern times, India's ruling classes were not generally keen writers; and, on aesthetics especially, they wrote extremely little, in spite of their central role as patrons. But such feelings about cultural alignments certainly existed among them, and were frequently observed by other writers. They were well illustrated, for example, by a conversation recorded by John Lockwood Kipling. When a Muhammadan gentleman of Bulandshahr built a house in an attempted classical style (fig. 18), and the local Collector, F.S. Growse, suggested that something more in harmony with national precedent might have been more appropriate, the proud householder replied: 'Such designs would be out of harmony with my own more advanced views, which are all in favour of English fashions. The trading classes do well to adhere to Hindustani types, but the landed gentry prefer to range themselves with their

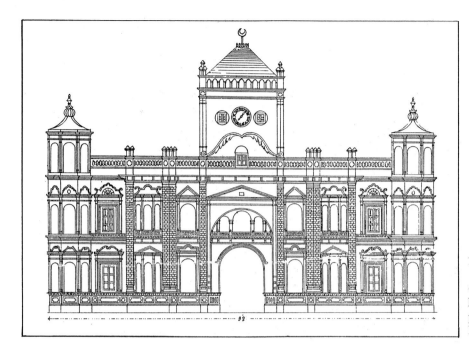

18. *Architecture as Understood by Native Gentry:* a view of a house in Bulandshahr, published by J. L. Kipling in 1886.

rulers'.[40] Similarly, E. B. Havell recorded that, when higher-class Indians wished to disparage traditional Indian craftsmen, the epithet they chose was 'uneducated'. Anything indigenous was associated with the backwardness of the lower classes. In the view of Indians, Havell supposed, an educated Indian engineer was one 'whose architectural qualifications are acquired by copying a few sheets of "classic" orders in Anglo-Indian technical colleges', and who built palaces for 'progressive' maharajas.[41]

It appears, then, that a number of related motives underlay the construction of a palace such as the Jai Vilas at Gwalior (fig. 15). In the first place, the treaties of the early nineteenth century created a climate in which fortified palaces on the traditional Indian pattern were no longer necessary, and there was a need instead for palaces suited to the entertainment of Europeans. Secondly, the widespread British contempt for Indian civilization, including architecture, created among the maharajas a reluctance to sustain old native styles, especially among those who did not already have long traditions behind them and so who had less to relinquish. Thirdly, the prestige attached to classical styles as a result of British building policy in India before 1850, ensured that it was classicism which filled the vacuum. And finally, the Government policy of Westernizing India's ruling classes reinforced the change in taste. In sum, the standards of civilization in India were now Western: Indian rulers built classical palaces to demonstrate that they were civilized.

In Gwalior, there were some striking local applications of these generalisations. Maharaja Jayaji Rao Scindia of Gwalior had occasion to be acutely aware of British power. In 1857, he had remained loyal to the British, but his troops had shown some inclination to sympathize with the mutineers, and in one of the most famous episodes of the mutiny, the Gwalior forces were led into battle by Scindia's neighbour, the Maharani of Jhansi. Consequently, the British invested the ancient fort of Gwalior, Scindia's principal stronghold, and were still in possession of it when he began to build his new palace on the plain. They gave the fort back at their leisure, nearly thirty years later. In the meantime, the Maharaja watched the British garrison paying scant respect to the ancient Hindu buildings within the fort: the great medieval temple, the Teli ka Mandir, for example, was put to service as a soda-water factory and coffee shop.[42] By such acts of desecration, the British showed Indian rulers how the ancient Hindu heritage was then regarded by those who laid claim to power and authority.

At the turn of the century, the Sikh Maharaja of Kapurthala, Jagatjit Singh, built a palace in the French Beaux-Arts manner and filled it with French furniture. By this means, he dissociated himself from the British and spurned their cultural influence. But instead of aligning himself with his own, Punjabi, tradition, he embraced another Western one, and one that the British would respect: indeed, the French was one civilization that a Briton might acknowledge as superior to his own. Thus the Maharaja of Kapurthala – more thoughtful or more vain than others – was able simultaneously to spurn the British and win their admiration.

If the sole standards of civilization in nineteenth-century India became those of the foreign conqueror, it would be reasonable to ask whether this had not happened before in a land so accustomed to being conquered as India. Between the late twelfth and early sixteenth centuries, northern India had suffered a succession of invasions by Muslims from Afghanistan and Central Asia; in the wake of those invasions, did the cultural standards not become Muslim? The answer is that they did to a degree, but the Muslim influence was much less pronounced and paramount than the British was to be. This is largely because the Muslims were content to be Indianized; they respected and sometimes adopted Indian ideas and values. Their own imported civilization was not offered as an immutable alternative, but was assimilated into the Indian tradition. And they formed no active policy of Islamization; their influence was passive. So although, certainly, there arose among Hindu maharajas a fashion for imitating ideas from Mughal palaces, the Mughals themselves were at the same time imitating Hindu palaces. The two traditions were respected on both sides sufficiently for them to interact constructively. Above all, a Hindu ruler did not have to abandon his own heritage in order to imitate Muslim ideas: it was not a question of substitution, but of adding to the range of cultural options. That Muslim values were not the only criteria of civilization was occasionally forcibly demonstrated, when a Muslim emperor chose – as Akbar did at Fatehpur Sikri – to adopt native ones.

In the eighteenth century, some Europeans in India similarly adopted Indian customs and styles; but perhaps even then it was more a matter of personal indulgence than Government policy, and certainly it was not sustained when the British began to rule substantially. Macaulayism did not offer a compromise between traditions; it offered not assimilation but exchange. The Muslim conquerors had been prepared to learn from the conquered natives, in architecture above all; the British disdained such assistance, and challenged those who would appear civilized to copy their building practices wholesale.

## Gothic

In the mid-nineteenth century, the cultural self-confidence of the British Empire in India wavered. No longer committed exclusively to classicism, its architects began to experiment with other styles. This led in time to attempts to find a new imperial style, attempts that ended in the development of Indo-Saracenic architecture. But earlier, architects adopted other styles that were already available. One such, of course, was Gothic. Never in the forefront of architectural developments, British architects in India were responding belatedly to the Gothic Revival at home.

The Gothic style had earlier been employed for the occasional church, such as St Peter's in the fort at Calcutta (1835), but it was not until the mid-century that it became fashionable for secular buildings. By the 1870s, according to Philip Davies, it had become the preferred choice for colonial bungalows.[43] The same decade saw major urban development in Bombay, with the construction of some magnificent Venetian Gothic public buildings, including the Secretariat and the Public Works Office, both designed by Henry St Clair Wilkins; the Law Courts, designed by James Fuller; and the Convocation Hall and Library of the University, built to designs sent out by George Gilbert Scott.[44]

In time, Gothic styles, like classical styles before them, found their way from British India into Princely India, as imitations of Gothic buildings began to appear in the autonomous Native States. The Maharaja of Mysore, for example, built a palace at Bangalore, modelled on Windsor Castle. And the process may be observed even in Junagadh, a small kingdom hidden in a corner of Gujarat. The local style of Junagadh, which flourished before the European influence was felt, may be observed in the tomb of a matriarch of the ruling dynasty, Maiji Sahiba, built in 1856-57 (fig. 19). Flimsy in structure and florid in detail (and in these respects illustrative of the decline of Indian architecture that preceded the European influence), it nevertheless shows craftsmanship of a very high order. Fergusson admired the carving but thought it better suited to wooden furniture than to a stone building and so chastised the 'want of propriety'.[45] Burgess was a little more enthusiastic, seeing in this and a few other tombs in the capital

the latest, and perhaps the last, purely indigenous specimens of architecture: for Public Works Officers and Italian workmen are doing their best to kill native art, and in the larger and wealthier towns of Gujarat with fatal effect, by erecting palaces for the chiefs, in a foreign style, badly imitated and unsuited to the climate or the age: and this example is rapidly being copied in less prominent places by native workmen.[46]

The prophecy was no sooner in print than fulfilled. The next royal tomb constructed in the city was that of Nawab Sahib Mahabat Khan (built 1878-92) (fig.20). This follows Indian precedent in its plan and in the form of the domes, but it makes ample use of Gothic forms: the trefoil arches are closer to Christian than to native models, and the clustered columns and much of the carving are similarly alien. Even the domes and baubles are grouped like the encrusted carving of Decorated Gothic. This is the Gothic counterpart of the classical formula achieved at Lucknow. The tomb was built at the instigation of the state's progressive Wazir,[47] named Bahauddin, who began life as a woodcutter and rose to prominence on the strength of his intelligence. His own tomb (built 1891-96) stands close to the Nawab's; it is more conventionally Indian in style, but it is surrounded by free-standing minarets, each of which is equipped with a spiral stair attached to its exterior surface, transforming it into a helter-skelter.

Anyone who has not visited Junagadh might be forgiven for supposing that it is fictitious: its very name might arouse suspicion (for it means no more than 'old fort'); images of its bizarre buildings do not make it seem any more real, and neither does the story of the woodcutter who became Wazir and introduced the Gothic style (and incidentally founded a college for the liberal arts). But no absurdity is inconceivable when British influence reaches remote parts of India. It was probably the same Wazir who was responsible for the programme of urban improvement that transformed the state capital, as if by the hand of a Nash or a Haussmann. Straight, broad bazaars lead through a sequence of arches to piazzas surrounded by arcades of shops, Italianate palaces and Venetian Gothic offices (fig.21); the city centre exudes a sense of order, urban splendour and civic pride, creating an effect not unlike Manchester. Junagadh had moved quickly from the interpolation of foreign details to the wholesale adoption of foreign styles. The choice of Venetian Gothic suggests that the immediate source of inspiration was Bombay, which was also the nearest major British centre.

The largest Italianate palace housed the main *darbar* hall. Inside, its copious ceiling is crowded with Venetian chandeliers, the floor is littered with chairs covered in beaten silver, and the walls are choked with darkening oils of over-dressed nawabs. Much of the other paraphernalia once housed in the palace – silver match-boxes and teapots, velvet fans, Chinese vases, stuffed tigers, and the rest of the clutter of Victorian princely civilization – is now housed in a museum in the city's Zoological Gardens.

19. Junagadh; the cenotaph of Maiji Sahiba (1856–57).

20. Junagadh; the cenotaph of Nawab Sahib Mahabat Khan (1878–92).

21. Junagadh; public buildings in the city centre (c. 1890).

## *Indo-Saracenic*

Another style that Indian rulers borrowed from their British imperial overlords was the Indo-Saracenic. British architects had developed this style as a result of a debate about the relative suitability of various styles to British building in India. The debate involved not only criteria such as climate and cost but also political considerations: it was in part a quest for a style which would be expressive of Britain's role in India. Some insisted that the style chosen, whether classical or Gothic, must be Western; that the mission of the Empire was civilizing and Westernizing in matters of law and education, and its architecture should reflect those same values. Others, arguing that the role of the Empire was paternalistic, wished to see the adoption of Indian styles, or the evolution of a style incorporating Indian features: something that the natives could relate to instead of being intimidated by. The details of this debate have been discussed elsewhere[48] and need not be repeated here; the present account is concerned with British building and policy only in so far as they affected native Indian tradition and taste. The debate was never resolved; the Public Works Department (the Government office responsible for almost all British buildings in India) remained dominated by aesthetic imperialists; but after about 1870, it did produce a number of buildings in attempted Indian styles.

These experiments were at the time, and have been since, described as 'Indo-Saracenic', a term requiring some explanation. The phrase was originally adopted by scholars such as Fergusson to describe the country's Islamic architecture, which is generally characterized by a blend of Indian and Islamic design ideas. For this purpose, the term was poorly chosen, for the Islamic element in the buildings concerned is not strictly Saracenic: India's Muslim conquerors were not Arabs but Afghans and Central Asians who drew many of their cultural ideas from Persia. But given the nineteenth-century association of the Islamic with the Saracenic, the term was clear, even if inexact, in its application to the architecture of the Mughals and their predecessors. And it was just that architecture which the British Victorian architects supposed they were reviving; seeing no need to distinguish their revival from its models, they gave it the same name. In fact, the revived style was far from authentic, and its distinct character ought to have had a distinct term. However, since 'Indo-Saracenic' has generally been dropped in its original usage (its absurdity there has been recognized and it has been replaced by 'Indo-Islamic'), it may continue in its secondary use without confusion. It does not at all describe the nineteenth-century buildings' style (which might more aptly be called 'Indo-Gothic'), but it has been so consistently in use since they were designed that it is convenient to keep it.[49]

Before about 1870, attempts by British architects to design in Indian styles were extremely rare. A house built in north Delhi by Sir Thomas Metcalfe in 1828 has a veranda of pointed arches around its colonial bungalow heart, but this is an unusual (and tame) precursor to the developments of the end of the

22. Bombay; Victoria Terminus, by F. W. Stevens (1878–87).

23. Madras; Victoria Memorial Hall (now the National Art Gallery), by Henry Irwin (1909).

24. Ajmer; Mayo College by Charles Mant (1875-85).

century. The adoption of Indian forms became easier after the arrival in India of the Gothic, for they could be grafted onto the Gothic frame, taking the place of that style's own rich ornament. This is how the Indo-Saracenic experiment began in Bombay, in buildings such as Victoria Terminus, designed by F. W. Stevens in 1878 (fig. 22), and the adjacent, more emphatically Indian, Municipal Building, designed by the same architect a decade later. A notably voluble proponent and eager experimenter was William Emerson, whose designs included Muir College in Allahabad (1870). But the Indo-Saracenic movement achieved its proudest expression in the work of Robert Fellowes Chisholm and Henry Irwin in Madras, where the former's University Senate House and Revenue Board Offices of the 1870s were followed by the latter's Law Courts and Art Gallery (fig. 23). Early in this century in Bombay, George Wittet inherited the mantle from Stevens, designing the Prince of Wales Museum in 1905 and the famous Gateway of India in 1911.

Again, the origins and development of the style in British India have been ably analysed elsewhere; what bears on the present discussion is its impact on native Indian taste and patronage. For, the new style was very swiftly adopted

48

25. Baroda; Laxmi Vilas, by Charles Mant (built 1878-90 under the supervision of R.F. Chisholm).

by some of the maharajas. It had for them a double advantage: on the surface, it was an Indian style and so enabled them to acknowledge their cultural roots, but it was at the same time an imperial style, with British sanction. It offered the maharajas a means of being simultaneously Indian and progressive. Generally, those who wished to adopt it employed the British architects who had developed the style. Thus, for example, Emerson designed a palace for the Maharaja of Bhavnagar in 1894, and Irwin designed the Amba Vilas in Mysore in 1900. In this, lies one of the major ironies of the period: by taking an interest in indigenous architectural forms, the British set an example which encouraged some maharajas to do the same, and thus the British were at last repeating the pattern established by their imperial predecessors, the Mughals; but the maharajas who were thus persuaded to return to Indian styles, looked not to local craftsmen but to British architects and engineers to supply them.

One of the most adventurous exponents of the style, and the one most taken up by maharajas, was Major Charles Mant of the Bombay Engineers. That the style had official British approval, and that it was considered suitable for use in the Native States, were both made clear through one of the earlier projects of

49

Mant's short career. This was Mayo College at Ajmer in Rajasthan, a school for Indian princes built by the British Government (fig. 24). In this building, the British actively introduced Princely India to the Indo-Saracenic style.

The school (which still functions, though it now caters to a wider clientele) had its origin in a scheme begun by Lord Mayo, Viceroy from 1869 to 1872. The intention was to educate young Indian princes as English public schoolboys, to turn them into English gentlemen. The school was part of the continuing policy of Westernization, and Mayo's original idea for the building was consistent with this: the boys were to be taught in a Greek temple. Dissatisfied with the designs that were produced, Mayo subsequently changed his mind in favour of the Indo-Saracenic.[50] This might be seen as a concession to the traditions of the Indian rulers, who were contributing to the cost and for whose benefit the whole enterprise was meant, but it was a limited concession: the chosen style was, after all, another imperial one.[51]

After the Greek-temple plan had been aborted, the project was handed to Mant in 1875, and the school's main building was constructed to his design between 1878 and 1885. It firmly established Mant as a leading practitioner of the Indo-Saracenic, and he was commissioned to design three palaces in the style: those of Kolhapur and Darbhanga, and the Laxmi Vilas for the Maharaja of Baroda in Gujarat (fig. 25).

Along with the Scindias of Gwalior and the Holkars of Indore, the Gaekwads of Baroda were one of the dominant Maratha houses. Sayaji Rao III came to the throne as a minor in 1875, and commissioned his new palace a few years later. In 1881, after having designed it, Mant died insane, and the now formally installed Maharaja brought another leading Indo-Saracenicist, R. F. Chisholm, from Madras, to supervise the palace's construction. It was completed in 1890.

As a ruler, Sayaji Rao was a reformer. He built roads and railways throughout his state, he outlawed child marriage and established free and compulsory education, he founded dispensaries and hospitals, and he revised the state's legal system. He even permitted a creeping democracy, with the formation of a legislative council. In all this, he was a typical Indian enlightened despot of his period, the sort of progressive maharaja who was ready to reform his medieval feudal kingdom, encouraged by the British, who sought to propagate the species (for example through Mayo College). It was these progressive maharajas who built the palaces of the new breed; for whether classical, Gothic or Indo-Saracenic in style, such a palace was a further mark of progressiveness. As Chisholm told the Royal Institute of British Architects in 1896: 'It must be kept in view that the native Rajas and chiefs of India are passing through a transitional period; that an old palace like that of Ambur would be about as useless to the present Gaekwar of Baroda as to an ordinary English gentleman.'[52] His new palace, by contrast, offered a cultural alignment with that English gentleman and his civilized values.

As Chisholm's remark hints, the Indian character of the Laxmi Vilas is no

26. Baroda; a palace interior (1899).

more than superficial. It is true that most of the individual forms and details on the building's exterior, and certainly the most visible, are Indian: the domes, the deeply curved *bangaldar* eaves, the balconies, the arches, the pierced screens and the mouldings are all faithfully copied from Indian sources. But these forms are combined in an entirely alien manner; they are taken as if from the pages of Indian architectural history and redeployed over the surface of an English country house. The building presents a lexicon of Indian architecture, but without the grammar.

The grammar, where the palace has any, is Western. Most obviously, the planning is Western. Although the palace retains the traditional threefold division – into public rooms, the Maharaja's private rooms and the *zenana* (or women's quarters) – the rooms themselves are spacious and open, following Western patterns of size and proportion. And they include state dining halls, billiard rooms and visitors' suites, all of which were unthinkable in an Indian palace of the preceding century. In matters of life-style, the Indo-Saracenic movement offered no compromise with Indian tradition; the Laxmi Vilas, despite its native dress, is as much one of the new breed as the Jai Vilas at Gwalior.

The interior reveals an obsession with Western things. Much of the marble used, for example, is not Indian; despite the loveliness of Rajasthani marble (which was used for the Taj Mahal), the Maharaja imported marble from Carrara. And twelve Venetians laid the mosaic floor in the Durbar Hall. The furnishings and ornaments in all Indo-Saracenic palaces were entirely European (fig. 26). The Laxmi Vilas was filled with French furniture; its walls were hung with large, indifferent oils depicting European landscapes, and with a collection of prints and copies after works by Angelica Kauffman – evidently at one time the Maharaja's fixation.

The ornaments in such palaces frequently included ingenious gadgets such as musical boxes and cuckoo clocks, often lavish improvements on the standard varieties, being made of gorgeous materials. The Indian maharajas had once been warriors, but now, forced off the battlefield by the Pax Britannica, they amused themselves with puerile contraptions custom-made by all the best firms of Bond Street.

When the Maharaja of Baroda required a Senate House for his state's university, the choice of the Indo-Saracenic style and of Chisholm as the architect were both entirely natural: the style had already been employed for an educational building in Mayo College, Chisholm had even designed a University Senate House in the style in Madras, and he had experience of working in Baroda. Chisholm's design (fig. 27) makes deliberate use of specifically local, that is Gujarati, forms. The pierced stone screens on the upper corridor, for example, are divided by mullions and transoms into square panels, each with a single large motif, and in this they imitate the *jalis* of the mosques and tombs built in the region in the fifteenth and sixteenth centuries. The red brick construction and the bands of green glazed tiles, by contrast, introduce a more Victorian note.

Among those who practised the Indo-Saracenic style and those who have written about it subsequently, there is a degree of uncertainty about its character and aims. On the one hand, it is sometimes seen as an authentic revival of Indian styles; it is supposed that, just as at home a Waterhouse or a Scott could revive medieval French or Venetian Gothic styles, so Mant and Chisholm and their colleagues were authentically reproducing Rajput, Gujarati and Mughal styles of the sixteenth and seventeenth centuries. On the other hand, their buildings are sometimes seen as achieving a fusion between Eastern and Western traditions, as presenting a new style created through a synthesis. These two approaches were so rarely distinguished that some individuals expressed both. Thus Chisholm advised architects in India to 'practise in the native styles',[53] but his remarks about the Laxmi Vilas, already quoted, indicate that he perceived a need for something that was not in fact entirely Indian. Mant combined both ideas in a single sentence: describing his design for Mayo College, he spoke of its 'Hindu feeling and treatment' but concluded that 'the whole building may be almost literally described, as being an adaptation of modern Hindu domestic architecture',[54] leaving one to ponder the relative force of 'literally' and 'adaptation'. Modern commentators – reasonably, in the circumstances – have simi-

27. Baroda; University Senate House (now the Faculty of Arts), designed by R.F. Chisholm (c. 1880).

larly wavered between depicting the Indo-Saracenic movement as an authentic revival and depicting it as an attempt at fusion.[55]

An elision of these two views is perhaps encouraged by the comparison with Victorian eclectic historicism at home. When European styles such as Venetian Gothic were put to new uses, they required less adaptation – because the original design principles differed less from those of the adapter – and so the adaptation could pass for an authentic revival. With Indian styles this was not the case, for their design principles differed fundamentally. In India, any adaptation that jettisons traditional planning principles can no longer be authentic revival, and any revival that preserves them is not a fusion of East and West. One cannot have a revival and a fusion at once.

Which of the two, then, is Indo-Saracenic architecture? It is neither. It fails as an authentic revival for the reasons already given: the planning and massing of the buildings are always thoroughly Western, and the revived Indian forms are merely sprinkled over a frame which is usually Gothic and sometimes classical. But neither can it properly be called a fusion, because there is no satisfactory synthesis between the two traditions. They are not resolved into a new architectural logic; some details of one are simply thrown over a structure of the other. The result is not a fusion but a medley, not a compound but a mixture.

The character of that mixture may more clearly be revealed by a comparison with other architectural movements. It has an obvious kinship, in the first place, with the essays in the Indian style produced in Georgian Britain. Both toy with Indian motifs while adhering to traditional Western systems of planning and proportions. Also, just as the Georgian buildings reflect a rise in interest in Indian architecture inspired by the publication of Hodges and the Daniells, so Indo-Saracenic buildings reflect the late nineteenth-century interest partly inspired by the work of Cunningham, Burgess and Fergusson; so that the Indo-Saracenic movement has its ultimate roots in the pages of Hodges and in the Royal Pavilion. The principal difference between the movements is that Indo-Saracenic architecture is earnest in intent, while the Georgian Indian style is usually whimsical. The exception in the earlier movement is Sezincote (fig. 17), which was designed not by a wit like Nash but by a band of *aficionados* including Thomas Daniell himself. The outcome is the most serious experiment of Georgian Indianism, its most committed attempt at authenticity, and also its greatest failure, since the authenticity was bound to be superficial. Those who describe it as an 'Indian country house'[56] ignore that there is no such thing, though they have found a phrase that aptly describes its unique inherent contradiction. Its seriousness renders Sezincote, of all Georgian Indian buildings, most like an Indo-Saracenic building such as the Laxmi Vilas (fig. 25): in both the Indian tradition has become a repertoire of decorative exotica with which to trick out an English country house.

This description points to another kinship of the movement, namely that with the fashion among nineteenth-century Indian architects for interpolating

Western motifs, as in the later architecture of Lucknow. In both cases, the essential pattern familiar to the architect has been preserved, but exotic details are hung over it; both entail the misunderstanding and consequent misapplication of a foreign tradition. The abuses of the Indian tradition perpetrated by Indo-Saracenic architects have been overlooked by recent English writers (often because those writers are themselves insufficiently familiar with the original Indian styles on which the exercises are based), but they are invariably present.

Consider, for example, Mayo College (fig. 24). This is a travesty of the Rajput domestic architecture on which Mant claimed to have based his design.[57] It is ponderous and solid, in comparison with its models which are notable for being light and airy. Here, the forms that should create lightness – the verandas, projecting balconies, and *chattris* – have become cumbersome; instead of opening up and giving depth to the facades, they have become great weights pinning them down. Furthermore, these forms are here evenly distributed over the facades: in Rajput houses and palaces, they are concentrated so that large, plain areas alternate with areas of intense ornament, where the balconies are piled one above another; this volatile rhythm was entirely missed by Mant, who evened the arrangement out to a dull monotone. More specific abuses are evident in certain details, including the tall, conical domes over the kiosks on the main front. For these domes are temple towers or *sikharas*, which in the Indian tradition are never employed over a *chattri* and never in secular architecture. Mant, like the architects of Lucknow, copied a form with no regard to its original significance or development. The senselessness of this abuse will not be felt by those not well versed in the Indian tradition, and it might be considered that the censure of it proceeds from a pedantic purism. Those who feel so might be less comfortable with a parallel abuse of the Western tradition: with the treatment of the cornice in the Kaisarbagh gate in Lucknow, for example (fig. 6). Such misapplications may be interesting as historical curiosities, but they are not good design.

If, however, these abuses are charitably supposed to be deliberate, rather than the result of simple ignorance, then they might be defended as the fruits of imaginative invention – a faculty which could reasonably be preferred to archaeological scrupulousness. Such a defence was in fact made by Chisholm in relation to his Senate House in Baroda, when he pointed out that the architect could either follow 'the comparatively easy archaeological road, copying piecemeal and wholesale structures of the past, or he may endeavour to master that spirit which produced such works, and select, reject, and modify the forms to suit the altered conditions'.[58] This is a just distinction, but Chisholm neglected to say that the mastery of the spirit can only come from a profound knowledge of the original, and that not every modification of traditional usage is masterly. The flexibility that is desirable is not a license for any and every alteration. Chisholm was right, that it is only through modification of traditional usage by masters of the spirit that architecture develops. Indian architecture had been developing in that way in the hands of Indian architects over the preceding two millennia. But the Indo-Saracenic architects often modified without their mastery; sometimes they were – as Fergusson described the Lucknow architects – illiterates copying inscriptions in a language they did not know.

Chisholm's Baroda Senate House (fig. 27) illustrates both kinds of modification. His redeployment of Gujarati *jalis* (customarily used in tombs to shade while admitting air) shows both sensitivity and invention: his *jalis* are not merely Orientalizing embellishments, for their function is preserved, while their setting and some aspects of their design (including their scale) are new. It could be claimed that Chisholm was here a master of the Indian tradition. But the *jalis* are used in conjunction with entrances on day-release from the Alhambra and domes snatched from Persia. It is as though Chisholm has taken three favourite pieces of Islamic design and quoted them together, in the hope that three fine things will add up to something trebly fine. They do not; they create only a collage. This is not mastery of the Islamic tradition; it is using that tradition as a store of riches, to be plundered without the impediments of taste and understanding.

In varying measures, all Indo-Saracenic buildings perpetrate abuses of this sort, unmasterly modifications arising from an insufficiently informed response to the attraction of exotic styles. But in spite of the similarities between this process and that which had been in operation in Lucknow, the results are generally better architecture than Lucknow's late buildings. There are various aspects to this higher quality. Firstly, though the Indian forms are often wrongly applied in such buildings, they are usually faithfully copied in themselves: whereas the Indian architect attempting classical design had only inferior and inexact classical models to imitate, the Indo-Saracenic architects could and did study the finest examples of Indian design; and they could engage Indian craftsmen to help them execute the details, relying on them for archaeological precision. Secondly, however unhistorically those details are grouped, they are often grouped with great panache. This is especially true of Mant's work: the monstrous main front of the Laxmi Vilas (fig. 25), five hundred feet long, takes the scissors and paste to every feature of the Indian tradition, but it is supremely picturesque and boldly dramatic.

But not even Mant mastered the spirit to a point where the Indian tradition became more to him than a new repertoire of decoration; and neither did he succeed, any more than his Indian counterparts in Lucknow, in fusing Eastern and Western traditions, as Indian and Islamic traditions had been fused under the patronage of the Mughals.

## Indo-Deco

The Indo-Saracenic style continued to be fashionable among maharajas well into the present century, though the formula changed in response to changing architectural trends in the West. The Indo-Gothic formula, which had been preferred at the end of the nineteenth century, was displaced in the 1930s by a comparable medley of Indian and Art Deco forms. In Baroda, for example, the buildings of Mant and Chisholm were succeeded by the Kirti Mandir, a royal memorial, where the Indian forms are rendered with a crisp angularity, and the murals by Nandalal Bose that decorate the interior have a fluid elegance. In another princely state of Gujarat, Morvi, a new palace was built between 1931 and 1944, in a wholly Art Deco style.

In 1935, the American architect Walter Burley Griffin, who had worked with Frank Lloyd Wright, accepted an invitation to visit India, to build a new library for Lucknow University.[59] Griffin arrived in Bombay (from Australia) in November of that year, and travelled slowly to Lucknow, visiting Gwalior and the Mughal cities of Agra, Fatehpur Sikri and Delhi on the way. While resident in Lucknow, he attracted a large number of commissions, but few of these were executed as Griffin died suddenly a year after his arrival, in February 1937. The few completed projects (all begun in 1936, and mostly in Lucknow) include the Pioneer Press, a private house, the buildings for the Lucknow Exhibition of 1937, and another private house, in Benares (the University Library was built to different designs). As a theosophist, Griffin was intellectually predisposed towards India; while there, he professed an interest in indigenous architectural ideas, and in their incorporation into his own designs. His Indian clients' preference for modern designs was a tendency which he thought 'understandable', but one to be 'vigorously combated'.[60] His designs – both those executed and those not – perhaps reveal something of this conflict of interests. With their heavy, cubic massing, relieved by bold bands of decoration, their dominant aesthetic is Art Deco, while Indian forms are employed to heighten the drama.

The finest example of Indo-Deco, however, is the Umaid Bhawan Palace in Jodhpur, designed by H. V. Lanchester and built between 1929 and 1944 (fig. 28). The forms are again crisp and precise, and the bland monochrome of the stone makes the eye concentrate on their carved shapes. The details of the exterior are mostly of Indian origin, and they evoke the spirit of Art Deco simply through their sculptural treatment and consequent chill elegance. The magnificent interior decorative schemes are more closely based on Western originals: the subterranean swimming pool, for example, is embellished with mosaics depicting the signs of the zodiac, and the Gemini twins, with their centre partings, have stepped from the pages of *Vogue*.

This palace has suffered a severe critical reception, but its character has generally been misunderstood. Lanchester himself explained that, 'in the architectural treatment and ornamental detail, any use of "Indo-Saracenic" features was regarded as inappropriate, in view of the fact that the States of Rajasthan only came to a very limited extent under Muslim domination'.[61] One critic, quoting this, concluded that the building is a mixture of 'civic monolithic' and 'a confusion of Renaissance mimicry' with little Indian detail.[62] This assessment entirely misses the point of Lanchester's remark and of his design: there is ample

Indian detail, but it is not 'Saracenic'; Lanchester eschewed Islamic forms for the historical reason given, and looked instead to an earlier Indian, pre-Islamic heritage. Thus the dripstones or *chajjas* are ribbed, recalling those of ancient Indian temples; and the dining hall is a reinterpretation of a Buddhist *caitya* or prayer hall of the first or second century. The exterior is entirely trabeate, except for the domes, and their concentric rings echo the stepped-ring construction of the local, medieval Jain temples.

What distinguishes these references to ancient religious monuments from, say, Mant's use of *sikharas* in Mayo College, is Lanchester's masterly invention. While most Indo-Saracenic architects adopted later Indian forms, Lanchester set himself the more difficult task of employing an archaic architectural vocabulary, but his handling of the Indian tradition is both more informed and more inventive than that achieved by his predecessors. He is never archaeologically scrupulous, but never illiterate either. The piers of the *porte-cochère*, and the *jalis* suspended between the columns of the outer veranda, cannot be traced to specific historical models; they are new designs, but they are drawn in the spirit of Indian originals. The planning of the palace, it is true, follows Western patterns, but Lanchester did not simply peg Indian details onto a Western frame, nor did he produce a scrapbook of Indian architecture; rather, examining that source, he designed new and powerful motifs. Among the essays in Indian styles by Englishmen, the Umaid Bhawan Palace comes closest to being a fusion of Eastern and Western traditions, prevented from being completely so only by its plan. Lanchester had progressed from toying with exotica and was approaching a new architectural logic. At the same moment, some Indian designers – like those responsible for the Ganga Niwas *darbar* hall in the Bikaner palace – were reaching a similar resolution; and the next moment, the curtain fell on the British presence in India.

28. Jodhpur; Umaid Bhawan Palace, by H.V. Lanchester (1929-44).

# CHAPTER THREE

# The Indian Revival

Just as the stylistic influence of colonial architecture tended to destroy traditional Indian design, so the changes in taste and patronage described in the preceding chapter tended to put the traditional Indian craftsman out of work. The fashion among maharajas for palaces of the new breed, many of which were designed by British architects, had the effect of depriving the native architectural craftsman of his traditional main source of patronage; and more generally, the Westernization of India's educated classes put all the native crafts in danger of extinction.

These developments were observed and deplored by a number of people. A part of the rhetoric of the Indo-Saracenic movement was that it would arrest the disintegration of Indian tradition, that it would sustain Indian architecture, and so fulfil an imperial obligation to the subject people. Lord Napier, praising the work of Chisholm in Madras, described it as 'the first example of a revival in native art, which I hope will not remain unappreciated and unfruitful'.[1] In fact, in the construction of Indo-Saracenic buildings such as Chisholm's and Mant's (figs. 24, 25, 27), the Indian craftsman was debarred from his traditional role quite as thoroughly as he was in the construction of great classical palaces such as the Jai Vilas at Gwalior (fig. 15). The problem was not only that the buildings were designed by Englishmen. The whole process of design and construction followed modern Western methods. As in any post-medieval European building, the design was determined by an individual designer, who worked it out on paper and then handed a group of drawings and instructions to workmen who executed them. This method was entirely different from the traditional Indian method, by which a co-operative group of craftsmen shared responsibility for both design and execution, and worked out both on site. The Indian mason or craftsman (*silpi* or *mistri*) was a member of a guild (*sreni*), and although individual members of a guild might be more or less dominant, no distinction was made between a designer and a builder. In the construction of the Indo-Saracenic buildings, traditional craftsmen were employed, but not in the traditional manner: they were made to work according to Western, not their own, methods. They were not involved in the design process, but employed as technicians to execute others' designs.

It has been claimed for Charles Mant that, on the contrary, he did involve Indian craftsmen in the designing, leaving all the details and decorations to them.[2] But this claim is contested by the records of Mant's habit of studying and photographing those details of ancient Indian buildings that he wished to introduce into his own buildings[3] – an effort which would scarcely have been necessary if he indeed relied on Indians for the detailing. That the Laxmi Vilas could have been built after Mant's death is itself a testimony to the Western method employed: the process of construction was merely a matter of translating into stone a design which had been previously determined and fixed on paper.

Similarly, R.F. Chisholm has been taken by some recent writers to have been a supporter of the Indian craftsman. This assessment relies on some remarks that Chisholm made in a lecture to the RIBA in 1883 concerning his Senate House in Baroda. He declared that the selection of an appropriate style concerned

> merely the paper part of the business. When the design is completed we have yet to deal with the work itself and with the workmen, the men who will actually leave the impress of their hands on the materials, and these men have an art language of their own, a language which you can recognize but cannot fully understand. For this reason an architect should unhesitatingly elect to practise in the native styles of art – indeed, the natural art-expression of these men is the *only* art to be obtained in the country.[4]

In other words, Chisholm urged the adoption of Indian styles, with Indian details, on the ground that the masons who would execute the design knew those and no other forms. Clearly then, he assumed that the role of the Indian mason was decisive. But it will be noticed that he spoke of the Indian mason as executor and not as designer; indeed, the mason was called in only 'when the design is completed'.

This restriction of the craftsman was perceived early in this century by the art historian E.B. Havell. Comparing the Indo-Saracenic movement with the original Mughal architecture on which it was supposed to be partly based, he commented: 'The engineer-architect does not come, as the Moguls did, to learn the art of building from the Indian master-builder but . . . to teach the application of Indian archaeology to the constructive methods of the West, using the Indian craftsman only as an instrument for creating a make-believe Anglo-Indian style'.[5] The shortcoming of the Indo-Saracenic movement as a revival of Indian crafts has been overlooked by many; but it was recognized, even before Havell, by a few others. They saw that whether or not it satisfied the British quest for an imperial style, and whether or not it satisfied the maharajas' quest for Indian palaces with Western amenities, it did not solve the crisis in Indian art.

They saw that the copying of antique styles did not give work to redundant craftsmen – at least, not the work for which they were qualified. In the 1880s, these people began to bring about another, more fundamental revival: one which handed responsibility for design back to Indians.

Among the prime movers in this revival were two British Government employees: Samuel Swinton Jacob, an engineer in the Public Works Department, and F.S. Growse, of the Indian Civil Service. In the last twenty years of the nineteenth century, these two men supervised the construction of a number of buildings in which the Indian guild system was permitted to function in the traditional manner.

Their efforts have not generally been distinguished from those of the Indo-Saracenic architects, and are even commonly discussed in the same context, as though they formed a part of that movement.[6] The elision is understandable: the line between the revival of style and the revival of craftsmanship is blurred, as already shown, by the rhetoric of the Indo-Saracenic movement, which appears to advocate support for the craftsman as well as for his styles. It is also blurred because Jacob and Growse occasionally did produce Indo-Saracenic designs, in addition to their other revivalist projects. But though blurred, the line is real enough: what was at stake was the survival of the Indian tradition; and the difference between those who claimed to be ensuring that survival while removing all responsibility from Indian hands, and those who sought to preserve the methods of the Indian guild system, was a significant difference – especially to the underemployed craftsman.

A third concurrent movement – and one with which Jacob and Growse were more closely associated – was the revival of Indian decorative arts and crafts. This was an attempt to purge Indian craft work of Western influence, to restore its traditions and to find new markets for it. Again, it was promoted by a few individuals: chiefly by Thomas Holbein Hendley (who worked closely with Jacob) and John Lockwood Kipling and Lockwood de Forest (both of whom were associated with Growse). The craft revival may be seen, in some measure, as a counterpart to William Morris's contemporary Arts and Crafts movement in England. There was not, in fact, any explicit connection: the Indian revivalists made little reference to Morris's ideas in their own writings, and they were responding to a crisis in India more than to a fashion at home. However, some of their more voluble supporters, such as George Birdwood, borrowed arguments from both Morris and Ruskin.

The following accounts consider the work of those who sought to restore the traditions and methods of the Indian craftsman, whether in architecture or the decorative arts, and to enhance the Government's confidence in his ability.

## Samuel Swinton Jacob and the Rajput Renaissance

Samuel Swinton Jacob was born into a dynasty of distinguished Indian army officers, which included the celebrated John Jacob of Jacobabad, a pre-mutiny adventurer who founded the irregular cavalry corps Jacob's Horse.[7] Samuel Swinton's own military career began with a commission in the Bombay Artillery in 1858, and he transferred to the Public Works Department in 1862. He did not remain long in the main body of that department: many of the maharajas ruling Native States established their own works departments and employed British PWD engineers on secondment; Jacob took up the post of Executive Engineer to the Maharaja of Jaipur in 1867, and he stayed in Jaipur until – indeed well beyond – his retirement in 1902.

Jacob was one among a number of Britons who worked in Jaipur in the late nineteenth century, in the employment first of Maharaja Sawai Ram Singh (r. 1835-80) and then of Maharaja Sawai Madho Singh II (r. 1880-1922). Rudyard Kipling (John Lockwood's son), who visited the State in 1887, explained the foreigners' role: 'When the late Maharaja ascended the throne . . . it was his royal will and pleasure that Jeypore should advance. . . . In the latter years of his reign, he was supplied with Englishmen who made the State their fatherland, and identified themselves with its progress as only Englishmen can'.[8] Apart from Jacob, the supply included the surgeons F. W. A. de Fabeck and Thomas Holbein Hendley, and other engineers. Between them, these men undertook a great deal of work, especially towards the development of medicine and irrigation in the State. But although in these fields (their main work), they were sure that the desired progress would come from the application of Western ideas, in matters of the arts (their main leisure), they were not convinced that progress meant Westernization. On the contrary, they were concerned to revivify the local arts by isolating them from Western influences. It was ironical perhaps that Sawai Ram Singh should have paid a group of Britons to undertake this Indianizing work while he amused himself with billiards, but it was a period well accustomed to irony.

The revival of Jaipur's arts began with the foundation of a School of Art in 1866. After a few years, the new school was put into the hands of Dr de Fabeck, who ran it until 1872 and gave it shape. There was an explicit intention that the Jaipur school should not follow the pattern of the Schools of Art that the British Government had established in the country's principal cities; for while the British schools gave instruction in the fine arts, de Fabeck's courses concentrated on local industrial arts and crafts.[9] The Jaipur school revived dying local crafts such as *koft garee* (the inlaying of gold on steel) and a blue and white pottery, which is still made in Jaipur today (fig. 29).[10] Certainly some of the crafts taught (such as electroplating and clock-making) were of Western origin, but most were purely traditional: they included sculpture, woodcarving, filigree, ironwork and embroidery. The courses in these crafts lasted up to five years, and were provided free to sons of the artisan castes; just over a hundred such pupils were registered in 1877, and over one hundred and fifty in 1916.[11] The instruction was given by Indian master craftsmen; indeed, the whole school was

29. Pottery vases from the Jaipur School of Art, illustrated in *Memorials of the Jeypore Exhibition 1883* (vol. 1, pl. XXVIII).

soon under entirely Indian direction, as Opendro Nath Sen was appointed its Principal in 1875 and continued in that office until 1907.

The work fostered by the school perhaps inspired, and certainly helped to make possible, the Jaipur Exhibition of 1883. This brought together craft works from all over India, though especially from Rajasthan, which were exhibited for two months in a newly constructed building close to the Maharaja's palace.[12] The purpose of the exhibition, in the words of its organiser, T.H. Hendley, was 'to present to the craftsmen selected examples of the best work of India, in the hope that they would profit thereby'. The majority of the objects were included because they were considered 'worthy of imitation', but Hendley also included some objects 'which show what should have been avoided, and what mischief has already been done by the contact between Oriental and European art.'[13] Most of the exhibits had been specially purchased, but some of the costlier items had been borrowed from neighbouring maharajas, and these items were photographed before being returned, so that a record of the Exhibition could be kept. For the intention had always been that the Exhibition should lead in time to a permanent display. When Hendley began to assemble items for the Exhibition in August 1881, he opened a small museum in temporary rooms, and the main part of the collection was eventually transferred to a custom-built museum, the Albert Hall, in the winter of 1886.[14]

Once established, the Museum was 'open, without admission charge, to visitors of all classes, between dawn and dusk on week days'.[15] Under Hendley's curatorship, it continued the main purpose of the Exhibition, namely to present Jaipur's craftsmen with the most exemplary specimens of the work of their pre-

64

decessors. Unlike the Exhibition, it also included some European works, so that the craftsmen could see what foreign artists produced, but Hendley took care that their inclusion was not misunderstood and made a firm distinction about them: 'No European forms are allowed to be copied; all good specimens of Indian artwork are freely lent to the local workmen for reproduction'.[16] As well as being a school for the craftsman, the Museum served as his shop window, for visitors were advised 'if they desire any special article to be copied to point it out to the demonstrator, who will place it at the disposal of the Principal of the School of Art for this purpose.'[17] The Museum also differed from the Exhibition in containing a scientific section. This part too was avowedly educational; but in the fields of zoology and anatomy, Hendley was not an enthusiast of native traditions, and he presented the Jaipur public with models and charts which he hoped would reveal to them the rudiments of true science.

The Museum was highly popular, receiving a quarter of a million visitors a year.[18] Rudyard Kipling described the enthusiasm of peasant visitors, and considered the whole building 'a rebuke to all other Museums in India from Calcutta downwards'.[19] Today, a considerable part of its original collection survives, though some insensitive additions have displaced much of the craft work; it is no longer true, as it was when Kipling saw it, that 'there is not a speck of dust from one end of the building to the other', [20] but the dust that has long settled on its South Kensington-style cases seems to help preserve this thoroughly Victorian institution.

The actual building was constructed under the supervision of Samuel Swinton Jacob, though that had not been the original intention. The idea of creating a museum and library for the city had first arisen in 1876. Jaipur was visited in February of that year by the Prince of Wales, who laid a foundation stone; the building received its rather unfortunate designation, the Albert Hall, after the Prince's first Christian name. No decision had then been taken about the building's design, and in the following year competition designs were invited by advertisement. Twenty-seven entries were submitted to the Maharaja, who pronounced none of them suitable, and de Fabeck was asked to prepare plans.[21] However, de Fabeck evidently fared no better, for after a year, he 'received a letter and remuneration from the Maharaja for his services up to date'[22] and matters were put into the hands of the Durbar, or state government. The Durbar did nothing for a while, and then was distracted by the death of the Maharaja in 1880. At this stage, nearly five years after the laying of the foundation stone, as Jacob recorded with a note of relief, 'I was asked by the Durbar to superintend the work'.[23] Under Jacob's direction, the Museum was constructed substantially in 1883–84 and formally opened in 1887.[24]

The exterior massing of the building (fig. 30), with its stepped form and receding piles of pavilions, recalls certain historical prototypes: the pyramid of pavilions was an ancient Indian form, revived in some early Mughal buildings such as the Panch Mahal at Fatehpur Sikri and Akbar's tomb at Sikandra, and echoed in Jaipur's own, early eighteenth-century City Palace. Otherwise, the building's arrangement, and especially its planning (fig. 31), is more Western than Indian, but this was natural for a museum, originally a Western institution. The main exhibition space consists of three long halls in one row; each is of double height and is provided with an overhanging internal balcony for pictures. In front of these halls are two open courts flanking a central large hall of uncertain function: Hendley declared sternly that it was intended for lectures and meetings, but a later commemorative album supposed that its wooden floor was designed for dancing and skating.[25]

The overall form of the building is perhaps not wholly successful, as the abrupt recession of the storeys leaves it without a dominating focus at the top. The exterior appearance is also marred by the treatment of the stone: it is cut into small blocks with a prominent mortar which tends to fragment the composition. However, the detailing, and especially the decorative stone-carving, is of a very high quality (fig. 32). This quality was both possible and felicitous because, as Hendley explained in his handbook to the Museum,

> Jeypore has always been famous throughout North India for the beauty of its carving in stone; but as the architect relied upon this important feature for the chief ornamentation of his building, it has not been thought necessary to illustrate this local art, but to direct the visitor's attention to the principal decorative examples in the edifice itself. [26]

From these remarks, it can be inferred that the decorative carving of the Albert Hall was designed, as well as executed, by the local craftsmen, for if it had been designed by Jacob himself then it could scarcely have been regarded by the Museum's curator as exemplifying a 'local art'. The same implication is contained, even more clearly, in Jacob's own account of this aspect of the Museum: 'The endeavour has been also to make the walls themselves a Museum, by taking advantage of many of the beautiful designs in old buildings near Delhi and Agra and elsewhere. In some cases designs have been followed; or have inspired the workmen here.'[27] Jacob had for some time been encouraging Jaipur craftsmen to study and produce measured drawings of the details of traditional buildings in the region, especially the great Mughal buildings of Delhi, Agra and Fatehpur Sikri, and the oldest buildings in Jaipur itself. This project led eventually to the publication of the twelve handsome volumes of the *Jeypore Portfolio of Architectural Details* between 1890 and 1913, but even before then it had begun to have the effect, sought by Jacob, of inspiring local craftsmen to work within their own traditional idiom. Hendley noted that those craftsmen who had spent a few months studying old buildings subsequently produced 'good designs, which are not copies of those originals, but really new creations of the same school'.[28]

It is clear that this is what was happening in the design of the details of the Albert Hall. The evidence consists not only of the hints contained in the remarks

30. Jaipur; Albert Hall, constructed under the direction of Samuel Swinton Jacob (1883–87).

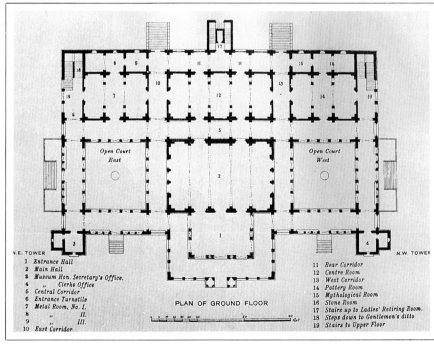

PLAN OF GROUND FLOOR

N.E. TOWER

N.W. TOWER

Open Court East

Open Court West

1  Entrance Hall
2  Main Hall
3  Museum Hon. Secretary's Office.
4  "  Clerks Office
5  Central Corridor
6  Entrance Turnstile
7  Metal Room, No. I.
8  "  II.
9  "  III.
10  East Corridor

11  Rear Corridor
12  Centre Room
13  West Corridor
14  Pottery Room
15  Mythological Room
16  Stone Room
17  Stairs up to Ladies' Retiring Room.
18  Steps down to Gentlemen's ditto
19  Stairs to Upper Floor

31. Jaipur; a plan of the ground storey of the Albert Hall, from *Handbook of the Jeypore Museum* (1896).

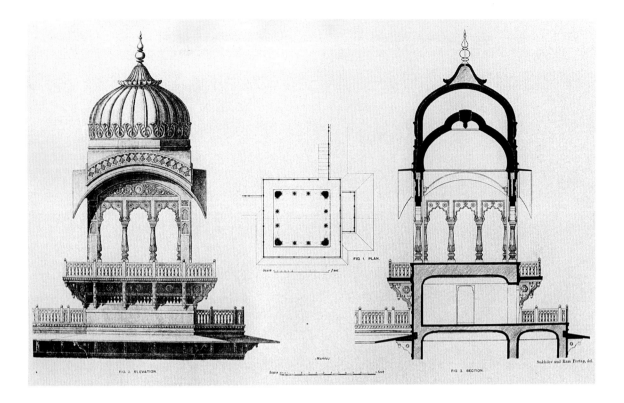

already quoted. Part XI of the *Jeypore Portfolio* (1912) includes, in addition to drawings of ancient buildings, some drawings described as 'designs prepared in Sir S. Jacob's office', and these designs – for free-standing *chattris* – are designated by printers' obelisks in the index; but the volume also contains a drawing of one of the corner *chattris* on the Albert Hall (fig. 33) and this is not so designated.[29] In other words, Jacob, while claiming credit for other designs, claimed none for the design of the most prominent features of the main front of the Albert Hall. Finally, Rudyard Kipling, who visited the Museum soon after its opening, described it as the work of 'Freemasons', noting that the masons chose the details; and though a journalist, the son of John Lockwood Kipling may be taken to be reliable on such a subject.[30]

This point is being pressed because it distinguishes the Albert Hall significantly from the buildings of the Indo-Saracenic movement. The Indian craftsmen were here not labourers executing a foreign architect's design; they were involved in the design and worked according to the inherited methods of the *sreni* or guild system. This perhaps subtle, but still crucial, distinction has generally been overlooked: modern writers have customarily mentioned Jacob only in the context of Indo-Saracenic architects; the Albert Hall has even been explicitly classed with George Wittet's Prince of Wales Museum in Bombay and Henry Irwin's Victoria Memorial Hall in Madras (fig. 23).[31] One writer has sug-

33. A *chattri* of the Albert Hall from *Jeypore Portfolio of Architectural Details*, part XI, pl. 12 (1913).

32. Jaipur; detail of the entrance to the Albert Hall (1883-87).

gested that Jacob's work differs from that of most Indo-Saracenic architects in being more authentic through being based on sounder scholarship;[32] scholarly Jacob certainly was, but the authenticity of the Albert Hall has another cause.

The oversight is the more surprising since we know the names of some of the Indian collaborators. An inscription at the entrance to the building attributes the 'superintendance' of its construction to Jacob, and the 'supervision' to Mir Tujumool Hoosein; it also mentions the draughtsmen Lala Rambux (Ram Bakhsh), Shankar Lal and Chote Lal, and the *mistris* Chander and Tara. These were only the principal agents: at the height of the construction process, the work involved, in addition to these draughtsmen and *mistris*, 182 stonecutters and 46 masons[33] (the distinction between these two groups being presumably one of skill and responsibility). The names given in the inscription are encountered again, along with others, in the reports of the State Public Works Department or other contemporary documents. Lala Ram Bakhsh, for example, is recorded as having been a pupil of the Jaipur School of Art; in 1877, he succeeded his brother as the principal instructor of drawing there, and he was succeeded in turn by Shankar Lal.[34] Other prominent Jaipur craftsmen included Ghasi Ram and Rup Chand, who worked as assistants in Jacob's office and stood in for him when he went on long leave in 1890.[35] And we encounter the names of many more craftsmen on the pages of the *Jeypore Portfolio*.

This last project was closely connected with the construction of the Albert Hall. The same annual report from Jacob's office that records the completion of the Museum's ground storey also records the production of some 'good and useful' drawings of 'old native buildings'.[36] By 1890, Jacob had collected enough of these drawings to issue the first six volumes of the *Jeypore Portfolio*. Published in London by Bernard Quaritch, under the patronage of the Maharaja, they contain measured drawings of plinths, columns, doors, brackets, arches and balustrades, of buildings mostly in Jaipur, Amber and the Mughal capitals, ranging in date from the sixteenth to the nineteenth centuries. The drawings are all by Jaipur natives, 'lads' trained in draughtsmanship first by de Fabeck and Jacob, and later by Ram Bakhsh.[37] Between 1894 and 1913, six further volumes appeared, covering string and band patterns, wall decoration, dados, parapets, *chattris* and *jarokhas*, from the same sources (fig. 34). In his prefaces to the volumes, Jacob explained that they were intended both as a record of historical examples and as a source of inspiration to the craftsmen. The drawings were issued loose-leaf, for ease of comparison, and on a large scale, because they were intended as 'working drawings'.[38]

This project arose partly from Jacob's dissatisfaction with the parent department to his own, the Public Works Department of British India. The PWD had been founded in 1854 by the then Governor General, Lord Dalhousie. It was responsible for the communications systems – the roads, railways and telegraph – and for all official buildings of the British Raj: not only the great public buildings of the Presidency towns (Calcutta, Madras and Bombay) but every courthouse,

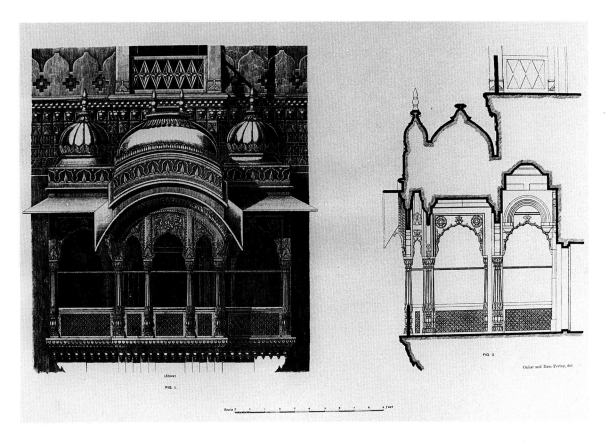

church, residential bungalow, school and collector's office, in every provincial
and district town. In view of this architectural emphasis, it is surprising that the
department should have been staffed not by professional architects but by military engineers. The more adventurous among them, it is true, became something like architects, and were responsible for the classical palaces and public
buildings of Calcutta and Madras, and the Gothic and Indo-Saracenic towers of
Bombay; for, whatever may be said regarding the success of these buildings,
they were designed with care and attention. But the same cannot be said of the
lesser and provincial buildings of the British Raj, which commonly display a
quite startling poverty of conception.

This was largely a result of the method employed. The PWD established
standard plans, so that all but the most important buildings were designed and
constructed according to fixed basic principles, merely adapted to meet particular needs. These standard plans offered, as it were, colonial bungalows off the
peg, with instructions about how they could be modified to make them serve
one function or another. An order of 1864 expressly forbade any deviation from
the standard plans.[39] They came in a variety of stylistic modes; the most common was a stripped and functional classicism (fig. 36), but there was also a

35. Agra; PWD bungalow in mixed style (late nineteenth century).

Gothic mode and a tame Oriental mode (a weak echo of Indo-Saracenic). Occasionally, jokey hybrids were attempted (fig. 35). The Indian builders who constructed these bungalows were often recruited from the *silpi* and *mistri* castes, and those in any position of responsibility had been trained in engineering in Government technical colleges, such as that at Roorki. The manner of their work departed considerably from their traditions, for, as designers, the most that they could hope for was to be involved in the adaptation of a standard plan.

Architectural historians were long hostile to the official buildings of British India, from Fergusson, who chastised the bungling amateur architects of Calcutta,[40] to Robert Byron, who famously described Bombay as 'that architectural Sodom' and observed more generally that 'the nineteenth century devised nothing lower than the municipal buildings of British India. Their ugliness is positive, daemonic'.[41] Rudyard Kipling summed up the more modest productions of the PWD more tersely with his term 'bungaloathsome'.[42] Some recent admirers of PWD work[43] have succeeded in raising understanding and appreciation of the major buildings in the Presidency towns, but they have not been able to excuse the dismal tedium of the lesser, provincial works.

A part of Jacob's aim in publishing the *Jeypore Portfolio* was to shake his colleagues out of their dependence on dull and uniform plans, to make them aware of the rich architectural heritage that surrounded them. He began his preface by quoting, from the guru Fergusson, a demand for greater public awareness of Indian design and the broadening of architects' minds. Jacob then continued in his own words:

> The Indian Public Works Department, as a body, has not hitherto been
> successful in its architectural efforts, and all who take an interest in

36. Agra; bungalow in the PWD classic mode (c. 1900).

architecture, and who know what vast stores of material lie scattered over the land, must regret the poverty of design and detail which, as a rule, characterises modern buildings in this country. . . . Standard plans are too often produced, and buildings are erected by men who have no sympathy with Oriental architecture . . . and hence . . . [we find] the stereotyped conventionalities which destroy all individuality. . . .[44]

Jacob's description of his book as a stimulus to the imagination and as a collection of 'working drawings for the architect and artizan' implicitly commended to the PWD his own practice of involving the Indian artisan in the design stage.

His labours were not noticed by the PWD, however, so much as by Rajput maharajas. In the later years of his residence in Jaipur, in addition to the work he did for the Maharaja of Jaipur, Jacob undertook a number of projects for the maharajas of neighbouring states. One such was Maharaja Ganga Singh of Bikaner, the northernmost state of Rajasthan, on the edge of the Thar desert. In many ways, Ganga Singh was a model maharaja. He was educated at Mayo College between 1889 and 1894, and under his rule his state enjoyed considerable advance in the fields of education, medicine, agriculture and communications. He founded a camel corps which served the British in Somaliland. His personal career was one of immense distinction: during the First World War, he fought in France and Egypt and was one of the signatories of the Treaty of Versailles; he served as the first Chancellor of the Chamber of Princes and subsequently represented his fellow Indian rulers at the Assembly of the League of Nations at Geneva in 1924, and at the Round Table conferences of 1930 and 1931; in the Second World War, he again took up arms, in spite of his years, fighting in the Middle East. He died in 1943 at the age of sixty-two. He was much admired by

37 Bikaner; Lalgarh, constructed under the direction of Samuel Swinton Jacob (1896).

the British, and collected honorary degrees and freemanships of cities by hand-fuls. Even an official publication of Independent India – and such works do not generally show sympathy with maharajas – acknowledges that 'the present Bikaner Division owes its prosperity entirely to his efforts'.[45]

As one would expect of a maharaja so loyal to the British Empire and to its re-forming mission, Ganga Singh required a palace of the new breed. One might expect to find in Bikaner, if not a heap of classicism like the Jai Vilas at Gwalior (fig. 15), then, maybe, an Indo-Saracenic concoction by Mant or Chisholm (figs. 24, 25, 27). And perhaps it was indeed something along Indo-Saracenic lines that Ganga Singh wanted; he went, after all, to a British engineer, and the choice of Jacob rather than Mant might have been due less to Jacob's ideas than to his presence in Jaipur, where he was close at hand.

If such had in fact been his wish, then in a sense he should not have been dis-appointed, for in some ways Lalgarh (fig. 37), designed by Jacob in 1896, fol-lows the Indo-Saracenic formula: the planning of individual rooms and their re-lationships, not to mention all their furnishings, fittings and decorations, are Western; and these Western rooms are contained in an Indian outer shell. But Lalgarh differs from Indo-Saracenic buildings in the character of that shell; for while the Laxmi Vilas, for example (fig. 25), is a scrapbook of Indian forms, torn from a wide range of Indian sources and re-arranged according to wholly

74

38. Bikaner; *zenana* apartments in the Anup Mahal Chowk of Junagadh Palace (late seventeenth century).

alien compositional ideas, the exterior of Lalgarh is designed in an authentic Rajput idiom. It is not eclectic but draws on local sources; indeed, not only is it purely Rajput in style, but with its extensive use of *jalis* and *bangaldar* eaves, it is typical of the regional variation of that style which characterizes Rajasthan's desert states, including Bikaner. Its main source of forms is the state's old fortified palace, Junagadh (fig. 38). The forms are arranged according to traditional compositional principles, too; the groupings of domes and balconies, for example, follow typical Rajput practice. It is no mere pastiche, for the application of Rajput facades to a new kind of plan required certain changes in scale and arrangement – openings, for example, tend to have been made larger – but in the process of adaptation, it developed the tradition with respect and understanding. It fulfils the ideal hinted at by Chisholm when he remarked that a mastery of the spirit of Indian design would enable and entitle an architect to 'select, reject and modify the forms to suit the altered conditions'.[46]

The overall form of Lalgarh is perhaps a little clumsy. Its regular court lacks Rajput picturesque whimsy. But much of the stone detailing is exquisite (fig. 39), and this relates to another point of distinction from Indo-Saracenic buildings: as a later collaborator with Jacob, Gordon Sanderson, recorded, 'all the details were worked out by native craftsmen'.[47] That mastery of the spirit, which enabled Jacob to fulfil Chisholm's ideal more completely than Chisholm could himself, was, it appears, in large measure borrowed; and the success of Lalgarh is a result of Jacob's willingness to give the craftsmen a free hand. From Sanderson's testimony, it seems that the division of labour in the design and construction of Lalgarh followed the pattern established in the Albert Hall at Jaipur, and indeed it achieves a similar degree of success. Jacob employed the same

39. Bikaner; a carved
window in Lalgarh
(1896).

method in at least two other projects: the Umed Bhawan in Kota, built for the Maharao of Kota in 1895, and the Judicial Court in Jodhpur (built 1893-96).[48]

These four buildings form only a small fraction of Jacob's work. Most of his energy was expended in providing the State of Jaipur with roads and irrigation. Even among his architectural projects, they are a minority and relate to a single theme of his work. He was involved in one way or another with almost every building constructed by the Jaipur State government in the four decades of his residence in Jaipur (and since it was a prosperous period, there were many such) in addition to several buildings outside Jaipur. He did not employ native craftsmen as designers in all his works. He was capable, for example, of producing buildings in wholly Western styles, such as the Early English All Saints' Church in Jaipur (1876) and the Scottish Baronial Secretariat Offices in Simla. He also produced a few genuinely Indo-Saracenic buildings, including St Stephen's College in Delhi and St John's College in Agra; though these handle the Indian tradition in a literate manner, there is no evidence of Indian craftsmen having assisted in their design (a circumstance perhaps explained by their having been the result of British, not Indian, patronage). He was even capable, in one instance, of the most horrendous variety of hybridisation, producing a design which jumbles Indian and classical motifs in the worst manner of Lucknow: this is the building on Jaipur's Sireh Deori Bazaar, originally called the Naya Mahal, which Jacob constructed to house the Jaipur Exhibition.[49]

Jacob's colleagues in Jaipur were similarly inconsistent. De Fabeck, who ran the School of Art in its formative years, was responsible for two Indo-Saracenic exercises: the Mayo Hospital in Jaipur (1870) and the State's boarding house in the grounds of Mayo College in Ajmer (built in 1873 to accommodate Jaipur pupils at the school). Hendley, the curator of the Albert Hall, devoted half that museum to the propagation of Western science; and though he was dedicated to the revival of India's industrial arts and crafts, he had (like his fellow enthusiast Sir George Birdwood) some harsh things to say about Indian fine arts, considering Hindu art 'conventional, and somewhat inelegant, or even grotesque' and Indo-Islamic art 'formal and rather childish' in comparison with 'pure and refined Greek art'.[50]

But even if they sometimes undermined their own efforts, Jacob, de Fabeck and Hendley did succeed between them in setting in motion a craft revival in Rajasthan, and one which continued for a while on its own momentum after their departure. Jacob retired from the PWD in 1902 with a knighthood; but he stayed on in Jaipur for a few years, initially to organize the Maharaja's visit to England for the coronation of Edward VII.[51] By this time, he could already see the beginnings of a sequence of buildings designed and constructed in the traditional manner, each with signs of his guiding, though remote, hand.

This sequence includes the Mubarak Mahal, a guest house built on the periphery of the Jaipur City Palace at the turn of the century (figs. 40, 41). There is no mention of this building in Jacob's departmental annual reports; and, given

40. Jaipur; Mubarak Mahal, constructed under the direction of Chiman Lal (c. 1900).

their thoroughness, it is clear that it was not the work of Jacob or his office. As a palace building, it ought to have been the responsibility not of the State PWD but of a distinct department, the Raj Imarat, which was specifically concerned (as its title implies) with buildings for the Maharaja. That it was indeed built by the Raj Imarat is indirectly confirmed by Gordon Sanderson, who published views of the building in 1913. Sanderson attributed its design to Lala Chiman Lal, who is elsewhere recorded as having been Darogha (director) of the Raj Imarat since 1886.[52] It was not built without Jacob's influence, however, for Jacob had taught Chiman Lal. And the building makes use of the *Jeypore Portfolio*, or of its method: some of its details are close to some of those published, without being replicas of them, suggesting that the portfolio drawings (or the original buildings) had served as a source of inspiration for new design (figs. 42, 43). Having been revivified by Jacob, the traditional *sreni* system operated once more in Jaipur, re-introducing methods some of which had been in use for millennia – for Sanderson recorded that, in the Mubarak Mahal, 'the ornament was sketched for the stone-cutters direct on the stone by draftsmen'.[53]

The Mubarak Mahal is a small, two-storeyed building, with rooms grouped around a central, double-height hall. It was originally intended as a guest house

78

where the Maharaja could receive and accommodate foreign visitors; later, it was occupied by the Durbar offices (the Mahakma Khas), and currently it houses a part of the Palace Museum. The plan (fig. 44) provides some satisfyingly related spaces; in particular, on the upper storey, a fringe of communicating chambers overlooks the central, open core, which was probably the main ceremonial space. This arrangement, together with the basic plan – a square subdivided into a three–by–three square grid – revives the theme of the *vastupurusha mandala*, the cosmological diagram that inspired the eighteenth-century planners of Jaipur city and had long been a motif in Rajput palace design.[54]

The greater beauty of the design, though, derives from the delicacy and depth of the facades (fig. 40). The depth is achieved by a number of devices: by the variation in the basic plan, with a veranda projecting in the centre of each side; by the cantilevered balconies, which project yet further; by the roof parapet, which rises above those balconies but is separated from them by a deep recession; by the pierced balustrade and the open arcade of the upper gallery. The open space above each arch in that gallery – an arrangement copied from traditional courtyard houses in the city – make the building's roof appear to float

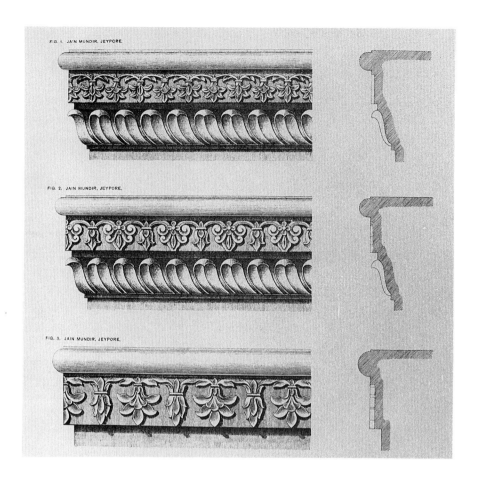

42. Plinths from a Jain temple in Jaipur, from *Jeypore Portfolio of Architectural Details*, part I, pl. 4 (1890).

weightlessly above it. The lightness and the depth are typically Rajput qualities: they can be seen in the ranges of the *zenanas* of the old Rajput palaces of Jodhpur and Bikaner (fig. 38), though they are here more pronounced. The carved ornament and delicate screenwork are similarly traditional. Though rich, they are not relentless: the projecting gallery is supported not on the more customary brackets, but on a smooth, curved moulding (derived from Jaipur's famous Hawa Mahal), which provides some visual relief and prevents the facades from being cluttered.

If the Mubarak Mahal thus reinterprets local sources (in a manner which Jacob would have approved), it is not entirely devoid of Western influence; but this is subdued and well assimilated. The tiny columns of the upper gallery are twisted and have leaf capitals, giving them a somewhat Romanesque appearance. The dado patterns on the interior are stencilled, applying a Victorian technique to Indian motifs. The aedicule doorways of the lower storey also suggest a Western influence: while their forms are Hindu, and the idea of an aedicule opening was not alien to the Indian tradition (as the niche in the temple wall had been trans-

43. Jaipur; detail of the plinth of the Mubarak Mahal (c. 1900).

lated into a window in fifteenth-century Rajput palaces), the aedicule had not previously been used for doors. Although this use represents only a slight further step, the result strongly echoes classical aedicules. The craftsmen could have observed examples of the classical form on Jacob's Naya Mahal nearby. If such was indeed their source, then these doors represent a new kind of Western influence: not the indiscriminate copying of motifs, but an intelligent adaptation of principles.

That the Mubarak Mahal is the only new building so far illustrated in this book that may unreservedly be admired, indicates the extraordinary difficulties which the cultural interactions of nineteenth-century India imposed on architects working there. It is not, however, unique. Facing it, to the north, and built at about the same time, is the gate known as the Rajendra Pol which leads from the Mubarak Mahal into the palace's major courts (fig. 45).[55] It shares many of the qualities of the Mubarak Mahal. The rich stone-carving revives and reworks traditional motifs, and provides a gorgeous surface which accentuates by contrast the gate's crisp main lines. A slightly later work of the Jaipur Raj Imarat is

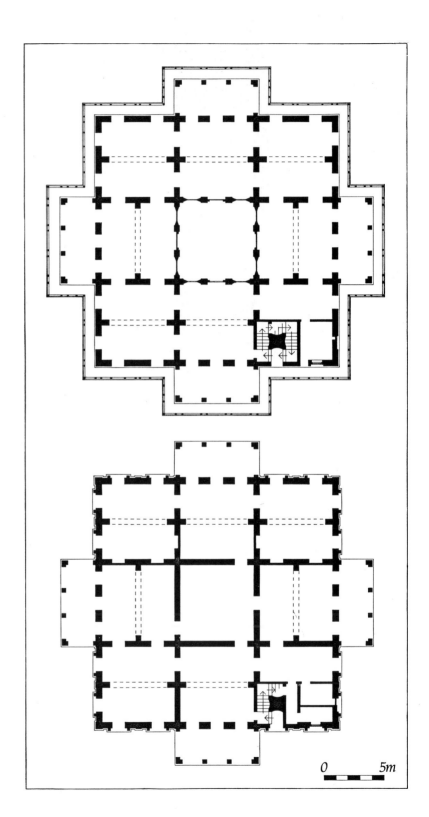

44. Jaipur; plan of the Mubarak Mahal: (above) upper storey and (below) lower storey.

0          5m

45. Jaipur; Rajendra Pol
(c. 1900).

46. Bikaner; Ratan
Bihari temple (1913).

the Memorial Sarai to King Edward VII; built in 1912, after Jacob's departure, it demonstrates that the revival could continue without its instigator.[56]

In Bikaner, too, some fine buildings followed in the wake of Jacob's Lalgarh, including the Ratan Bihari temple (1913) (fig. 46) and the High Court (1915).

These buildings are more spacious in their planning and more advanced in their engineering than their medieval antecedents, from which they otherwise draw their vocabulary, but these are the only aspects of a cautiously admitted Western influence. Half a century after the enthusiastic but unconsidered experiments in Lucknow, a few Indian architects had learned to take what was useful from the West while retaining their own language.

## F.S. Growse, 'Apostle of Culture'

At the same time that Jacob was working in Jaipur, some similar projects were undertaken in Mathura and Bulandshahr – provincial districts between Delhi and Agra – by Frederick S. Growse. Jacob and Growse evidently knew of each other's work (Growse lent some items to the Jaipur Exhibition), but their efforts were not coordinated. Indeed, there were some important differences between the two men. Growse was a member not of the Public Works Department but of the Indian Civil Service, and he worked not in a Native State but in British India. It was this latter difference rather than his lack of training as an engineer which impeded his revival work, however, because instead of being (like Jacob) answerable only to a sympathetic autonomous ruler, he found himself in conflict with various British authorities, including the central PWD.

After being educated at Oxford, Growse went out to India to join the ICS in 1860. That service contained many men of fine intellect, but few with his antiquarian and scholarly interests. There was therefore a certain fitness in his posting, in 1870, to Mathura, the ancient holy Hindu city on the Yamuna just north of Agra. While in Mathura, he published a translation of the Hindi version of the *Ramayana*, founded a museum, and published the first edition of *Mathura: A District Memoir*. This last is one in a uniform series of local histories published by the Government, but Growse's volume is distinguished from most by his depth of learning and knowledge of local history. It is further distinguished by a belligerence towards authority, especially on academic points: in the preface, he deplored the officially approved spelling of the city's name, remarking that

> the place has had an historical existence for more than 2,000 years, and may reasonably demur to appearing in its old age under such a vulgar and offensive form as 'Muttra', which represents neither the correct pronunciation nor the etymology. . . . But this is a subject upon which, as my own personal views are not in accord with those of the local [district] Government, it would be out of place for me here to enlarge.

That these comments were a deliberate and personal affront to a superior is evident from a footnote added to the preface in the book's second edition: 'At the time when this was written, Sir William Muir, a most obstinate supporter of the old haphazard mode of spelling, was the Lieutenant-Governor of the North-West'.[57] What this complaint reveals (apart from Growse's preference for a method of transliteration with which modern scholars agree) is his readiness to engage in unequal combat and his contempt for those who were his intellectual inferiors, even when they happened also to be his professional masters.

These qualities were soon to lead him into a more serious tussle with a more lasting opponent: the Public Works Department. Like Jacob, Growse objected to the dullness of PWD standard plans, and to that Department's refusal to employ skilled local craftsmen as anything but executors of those dull plans. But he was even more radical than Jacob in his view of the Indian craftsman's potential role:

> I have never been able to understand why a large and costly staff of European engineers should be kept up at all, except for such Imperial undertakings as Railways and Canals. The finest buildings in the country date from before our arrival in it, and the descendants of the men who designed and executed them are still employed by the natives themselves for their temples, tanks, palaces, and mosques. If the Government utilized the same agency, there would be a great saving in cost and an equal gain in artistic result.[58]

The construction of a new Catholic Church in Mathura (begun in 1874) gave Growse the opportunity for his first major exercise in employing local craftsmen and involving them in architectural design. The result (fig. 47) is a tentative essay and far from a fulfilment of all his aims. He did not leave the detailed design entirely to the craftsmen; his own guiding hand was somewhat heavy, and

47. Mathura; Church of the Sacred Heart, constructed under the direction of F.S. Growse (1874-78).

85

the result is correspondingly clumsy. Most of the details are Indian, and they were executed by native masons, but Growse selected and arranged them. He originally intended the church spire to be in the form of a Hindu temple *sikhara*; but, anxious not to cause offence to the clerics, he compromised with a Russian style of dome, since that is also Eastern. He later conceded that the compromise marred the design.[59]

The Catholic Church succeeded in one regard, however. As Growse happily recorded, it annoyed the PWD:

> An Executive Engineer, attached in some subordinate capacity to Government headquarters – in retaliation for my frequent criticisms on the productions of that chartered anti-aesthetic society of which he is a member, and the destructive influence of which on native art I have done my utmost to expose – employed himself at intervals under a variety of assumed names by filling columns of the *Pioneer* with tirades against 'the dreadful Mathura chapel'. . . . I intended the building to be a protest against the 'standard plans' and other stereotyped conventionalities of his department; and the indignation it has excited shows that it is accepted in that light.[60]

He was not able to supervise the completion of the work, for his combative manners provoked authority, and in 1878 he was abruptly transferred from Mathura and appointed Collector of Bulandshahr, the principal town of a small district south of Delhi. That this move was definitely a demotion did not deter Growse; during his six years in Bulandshahr, he stepped up his attacks on the PWD and initiated major building programmes in defiance of its approved methods.

At the time of his transfer, he was already engaged on a second edition of his district memoir; he was permitted to complete this, and it was published in 1880. Even more than the original edition, it is full of scholarly diversions, such as a lengthy consideration of an etymolgy or an iconographical analysis of a piece of sculpture. It is also full of resentment: he complained that certain of his projects in Mathura – including the establishment of the museum and the restoration of the temple of Brindaban, as well as the building of the Catholic Church – were dropped the moment he left.[61] The PWD features largely, in the role of principal demon. Growse declared that his intention had been to include, in the museum, models of good local buildings for the instruction of apprentice masons, together with one of a PWD building as 'a model of everything to be avoided'; he told tales of the philistinism and folly of PWD engineers who were careless of Indian monuments; and he contrasted his own 'efforts to develop native talent' with 'the efforts of the Engineers to extinguish it'.[62]

His own efforts were meanwhile beginning to bear fruit in his new environment at Bulandshahr. When he arrived, he found it an unremarkable town, without beauty or dignity. The main square, or *chowk*, was an untidy waste-

land. Growse had this space cleared and provided with a shallow podium, to separate the central area from the surrounding streets; at one end of the podium was erected a *piyao*, a shelter from which water could be dispensed to passers-by. The improved *chowk* was then bounded by fine new ranges of buildings. Among these, the most impressive is that on the east side (fig. 48); built in 1880-81, it contains a Hindu temple (at the northern end) and a three-storey house built for a leading Muslim merchant named Saiyid Mihrban Ali Galaothi. The whole range is faced in the local buff sandstone and is richly ornamented with carving and pierced screen-work (fig. 49); the symmetry and delicacy of this decoration are set off, in a traditional manner, by the irregularity and power of the range's massing.

The rebuilding of the *chowk* was only the beginning. Growse subsequently provided the town with numerous gates (such as the gates to the municipal garden), a town hall, and a tank with bathing *ghats* (steps leading into the water). He also arranged for the building of similar structures in Khurja, the next largest town in the Bulandshahr district. Khurja was a trading town, and Growse persuaded its merchants to rebuild their market and provide it with a handsome gate (fig. 50). This structure is sixty feet deep behind its elaborate facade, and its

48. Bulandshahr; range to the east of the *chowk*, with the temple entrance at left (1880-81).

stateliness earned it, among the merchants, the sobriquet 'Badshahi Imarat' (or 'sultan's building'), implying a kinship with the buildings of the Mughals and – as Growse had it – 'thus expressing the contrast they presented to the cramped and skimpy inanities of our professional engineers'.[63]

Growse had a smaller personal role in the design of all these buildings than he had had in that of the Mathura Catholic Church; indeed, his role was probably even slighter than Jacob's had been in the design of the Albert Hall. He made arrangements for the buildings' construction, and for the payment of the crafts-men. It is clear that he was also in some measure involved in the design: he re-marked of a house in Khurja that he had 'no personal responsibility whatever' for it, thus distinguishing it from the buildings whose construction he had supervised.[64] However, this supervisory role seems to have consisted primarily in persuading the native craftsmen to adhere to their own traditions and not attempt to introduce Western forms. Growse did not altogether disapprove of putting foreign elements into a design, provided that they were well assimi-lated, but he did not encourage the practice: 'I am far more conservative of Oriental tradition in the buildings I supervise than my workmen would be if they were left entirely to their own devices'.[65]

The implication in this remark, that Growse's role was essentially advisory, is reinforced by the assertion of Purdon Clarke (one of Growse's earliest de-fenders), that the Bulandshahr buildings were 'designed by good native work-men, the only European influence exercised being Mr Growse's criticism'.[66] It is highly probable that Growse did not put pencil to paper; and if this seems an in-credible restraint, it should be remembered that he was not trained to do so (no doubt he had in the design of the Mathura church, but he was among the first to call the result a failure). The measured drawings that he later published (fig. 50) are all the work of Indian draughtsmen. And finally, as with Jacob's projects, we know the names of some of the individual Indian *mistris* who were involved: Growse recorded that the stone screens of the Galaothi house (fig. 49) were de-signed by two brothers, 'Yusuf and Mirchu, of Mathura, whom I have employed as headmen in all my operations'.[67] In spite of this, Growse has some-times been associated with Indo-Saracenic architects; he has even been accused of having sought, in his writings, to publicise 'his own work'[68] when, on the contrary, his whole case was that Indian work is preferable to anything English-men might produce.

Though close to Delhi, Bulandshahr has never been metropolitan, and Growse's projects were unlikely to attract a large audience. To Growse, merely demonstrating the viability of his proposals was not enough; he wanted the demonstrations to be widely noticed. In the later edition of his district memoir, he declared an intention to produce a book illustrating all his architectural pro-jects, so that a wide public could weigh the relative merits of his efforts and PWD policies. Such a work duly appeared as a pamphlet in November 1884. Before that month was out, Growse received another notice of transfer, this

49. Bulandshahr; detail of the facade of the house of Saiyid Mihrban Ali Galaothi (1880–81).

50. The Main Gate, Khurja Market Place; *mistri*'s drawing published in *Indian Architecture of Today*, pl. xxvii (1886).

time to a yet smaller backwater named Fatehpur. Growse found little to distinguish this town among the many others of the same name, though he found it 'a charmingly quiet spot for a dead man to be buried in'.[69] Again, he had challenged authority and had been punished. But in the quietness of Fatehpur, he had time to work on a second, expanded, two-volume edition of his polemic, re-titled *Indian Architecture of Today as Exemplified in New Buildings in the Buland-shahr District;*[70] in this book, Growse reflected on the motives that underlay his work and on the conflict into which it drew him.

He stated that his two primary aims had been to improve the taste of – that is, to re-Indianize – the native gentry, and to provide employment for impover-ished craftsmen; he had further hoped to demonstrate the craftsmen's ability and, indeed, the economy of employing them.[71] It was PWD practice not to employ any Indian craftsman unless he had studied at the Government's Roorki College of Engineers. The stated reason for this policy was that, until he had studied at such a college, the Indian craftsman did not understand enough English even to keep accounts. Growse objected that the policy ensured that buildings were constructed by men who might be able accountants and linguists but were unlikely to be good designers:

> The *mistri*, or indigenous architect, thus superciliously excluded from competition, may be a skilled craftsman, whose work is of sufficient merit to be transported at great expense across the sea and set up for admiration in New York or London; but in India he cannot be trusted to design or carry out the most petty work in the smallest village: the reason being that he has spent the whole of his life in acquiring a practical mastery of his art and therefore has had no time to study English and technical accounts. Any native of ordinary ability can learn English and in due course obtain an Engineering certificate; having done so, he is at once qualified for an appointment of Rs 250 a month, in which he will be freely entrusted with the design and execution of local works, though he may know nothing of architecture beyond the hideous 'standard plans' provided by the Public Works Department.

To such torrents of rhetoric, Growse habitually appended penetratingly simple solutions: 'It would surely be more reasonable to pay the skilled *mistri* Rs 200 and engage an [English-speaking] assistant at Rs 50 to enter figures, thus getting both work and accounts done well for the Rs 250 now paid for incompetence.'[72] This argument was ignored by the PWD, as it was bound to be, since (as Growse knew) the stated objection to the *mistri* concealed a profound aversion to the appearance of Indian architecture within the department. As Growse noted, Roorki College was a place 'where no Orientalism has ever been tolerated'.[73]

It was because he was aware of this aversion – one not amenable to logic – that Growse had bypassed the PWD and organized building work in his district him-self, giving commissions to the local *mistris*. He knew that in art, fashion is para-mount; his hope was that he would persuade the local Indian gentry to follow his lead, and so give the craftsmen a wider source of patronage. He was temporarily successful in this, but, as he sadly recorded, the abruptness of his transfer from Bulandshahr thoroughly discredited his actions, and the gentry immediately re-verted to taking their guidance in artistic matters from the PWD. One of their number, for example, sent to Growse (whether to torment him in his exile, or innocently supposing it would give him pleasure, is not known) a photograph of the gate he had lately added in front of his house; Growse observed the '8 huge Doric pillars of plastered brick' and realized that the patron once again preferred 'the clumsiest travesty of a foreign model to the most graceful conception of home growth'.[74]

Before his second transfer, Growse was called on to defend himself for having arranged building projects without the sanction of the PWD. His defence was that all of the works had been built for the general good and had been paid for by the local gentry; an exception to this was the Mathura Church, for which Growse had paid a large part himself.[75] Next, the work itself was objected to. It was suggested that construction undertaken by Indian masons not trained by the Government would not be sound; Growse replied that one of the bathing *ghats* constructed under his supervision had withstood flooding better than a PWD work on the same river. It was also assumed that the Indian *mistri*'s work, being highly ornamented, was expensive; and when Growse showed that he could not be accused of extravagance with public funds (since he had not used any), he was accused of inciting the local gentry to extravagance.[76] In fact, as Growse repeatedly pointed out, the work was not expensive; though ornamented, the *mistri*'s products were actually cheaper than PWD work. In brief, Growse could claim that native work was 'cheaper, more substantial, and more artistic than that turned out by the department'.[77]

Growse did not wish to see the complete disbandment of the PWD; he merely wished to see it restricted to those things that it was good at, such as roads, with architecture left to Indians. It is perhaps not to be wondered at that the engineers objected to this civil servant who presumed to teach them their own profession, and who suggested that the natives might do better. But when the order of transfer came, on 28 November 1884, it made no mention of architecture. The official reason given for his dismissal from Bulandshahr was his disagreement with Government policies relating to local revenue administration and occupancy rights. Sir Alfred Lyall, the Lieutenant Governor of the Province, objected to the astringent prose style in which Growse had expressed his reservations. This seems a tame matter, and certainly Growse believed that it merely offered the Government a pretext, and that his architectural projects were the true cause of his transfer.[78]

Even if by proxy, the PWD had won. Ultimately, as Growse reflected bitterly, he had brought the craftsmen of Bulandshahr more harm than good:

> I was moved so suddenly that it was impossible for me to wind up their accounts, and since I have left they have experienced the greatest difficulty in getting paid for the work which they stayed on to finish . . . while – to complete the frustration of all my hopes for their advancement – a circular has lately been issued which preremptorily forbids their employment under Government.[79]

By New Year 1885, Growse was in Fatehpur, a town distinguished by 'a total want of skilled artisans'.[80] Even there, he endeavoured to stimulate craft work, but he did not last much longer: in 1889, he resigned from the service and left India. The self-proclaimed 'apostle of culture'[81] had attempted to open the eyes of a philistine society, but achieved only martyrdom.

## Industrial and Decorative Arts

Though not prepared to trust him with architecture, the British Government in India was not entirely insensitive to the plight of the craftsman, and some efforts were made to support him in the fields of the industrial and decorative arts. These efforts were not always consistent and properly considered, but they were well-intentioned. Even before the Sepoy Mutiny, for example, it was perceived that India's manufacturing crafts were under threat from cheap and novel imports from Europe; and in 1853, on the suggestion of Sir Charles Trevelyan, the Government founded a School of Art in each of the Presidency towns and in Lahore, expressly to counteract this process by giving encouragement to indigenous arts. In practice, these schools tended to be Westernizing, as the pupils were instructed in classical figure drawing and presented with Gothic decoration to copy; and if anything hampered that tendency, it was only the total lack of interest on the part of many officials.

In Europe, however, interest in India's crafts was growing and was reflected in a spate of exhibitions. Objects of Indian manufacture had been included, of course, in the Great Exhibition of 1851, and subsequently the Paris Exhibition of 1867 also had an Indian section. In the 1870s, a number of exhibitions of Indian art were held in London, especially through the South Kensington Museum. Closely involved with several of these exhibitions was Sir George Birdwood, who became a keen defender of India's crafts and renewed the appeal for help. In his work of 1880, *The Industrial Arts of India*, Birdwood charted the demise of India's craft traditions. He chastised Indian maharajas who adopted Western styles and ceased to patronize indigenous arts, and he foretold that the increasing industrialization of India would further deprive the craftsman of patronage and force him to become a factory hand. He deplored Western stylistic influence on the crafts that had survived:

> Indian collections are now also seen to be more and more overcrowded with mongrel forms, the result of the influences on Indian art of European society, European education, and above all of the irresistible energy of the mechanical productiveness of Birmingham and Manchester. Through all these means foreign forms of ornament are being constantly introduced into the country; and so rapidly are they spreading, that there is a real fear that they may at last irretrievably vitiate the native tradition of the decorative art of India.[82]

Before his return to England in 1868, Birdwood had been a distinguished doctor and public servant in India; he was not a man whom the Government in India could easily ignore, especially since his ideas coincided with those of William Morris, whose Arts and Crafts movement was then so fashionable at home.

A final spur to action, perhaps, was provided by the Jaipur Exhibition of 1883: in the matter of promoting Indian crafts and purging them of Western influence, the lead in India was taken in a Native State. But the Government followed swiftly, and in the month following the Jaipur Exhibition, passed a Resolution declaring that it was Government policy to promote Indian craft products and to increase public understanding of them.[83] The Resolution announced intentions to broaden the scope of the Schools of Art by admitting craftsmen as well as artists, and to stimulate a market for Indian crafts both among the maharajas (who were to be persuaded to finance the schools) and at home. It suggested that new markets might be found through the adaptation of Indian artefacts to Western needs, and expressed a hope that the Westernization of indigenous traditions could be arrested (without, however, considering how those two aims were to be reconciled). But if parts of it were confused, the Resolution nevertheless showed that the Government had taken note of the situation.

Growse professed to be puzzled about how a government that claimed concern for the craftsman and expressed a wish to find him patrons, still refused to allow him to design buildings. He knew, though, that the problem lay in departmentalism: in matters of building, all authority rested with the PWD, and if this department chose to pull in a different direction from others, there was nothing to prevent it from doing so.[84] This was the more unfortunate, since some of India's crafts, such as stone-carving and woodwork, were closely associated with architecture – indeed, traditionally they were inseparable from it – and so, without a change in the policies of the PWD, these crafts could not benefit fully from the Resolution.

A positive product of the Resolution, however, was *The Journal of Indian Art*, the first number of which was issued in October 1886. This was intended to fulfil two of the Resolution's aims: to increase understanding of Indian crafts, and to stimulate a market for them in the West. The *Journal* was to be a sort of catalogue of Indian arts (figs. 51, 52). Its most frequent early contributor was John Lockwood Kipling, who became a leading figure in India's craft revival.

Kipling had begun his artistic career in England as a sculptor and pottery modeller. In 1865, he went out to India to take up a post at the Bombay School of Art. As remarked, the policies of such Government schools were not conducive to the support of indigenous traditions, and though the work which Kipling undertook in Bombay is sometimes cited as an example of revivalist concerns,[85] it was in fact nothing of the sort. His work was to train Indian sculptors to execute the decoration of Bombay's great Indo-Saracenic public buildings; and while this certainly gave employment to native sculptors, it did not revive their traditions, for it taught them to work from paper instructions rather than from

51. Modern door carved
in deodar at Bhera,
Punjab; published by
J.L. Kipling in *The
Journal of Indian Art*
(1886).

52. *Pinjra* or geometric work in wood, Punjab; published by J.L. Kipling in *The Journal of Indian Art* (1886).

their own imaginations. His revivalist work began only after his appointment in 1875 as Principal of the Mayo School of Art, in Lahore. There he became interested in the local (Punjabi) wood-carving tradition. He published information about it (figs. 51, 52) and undertook a number of projects to revive it without taking the responsibility for design to himself. At one point, in 1890, as already observed, he transported a Punjabi craftsman to the Isle of Wight to work on a dining room for the Empress.

Kipling's interest in wood-carving was partly inspired by his meeting in 1881 with a visiting American designer, Lockwood de Forest, who was a member of the New York design studio, Associated Artists (which included Louis Comfort Tiffany).[86] In 1881, de Forest travelled to India in search of examples of traditional wood-carving, to inspire him in his interior-design schemes. He visited the city of Ahmedabad, which had been a centre of wood-carving for several centuries (in spite of being in a region devoid of trees, so that the wood had to be imported). De Forest found there a number of craftsmen, and this encounter – together with his meetings with Kipling and Growse – inspired him to establish a business, the Ahmedabad Woodcarving Company, which produced carvings for export to America. The company made decorative panels and furniture, to be integrated into Associated Artists' interiors. It was important to de Forest that the craftsmen should adhere to their traditional methods and forms; it was not a question of adapting their craft to the American market so much as adapting American taste to the Indian product. Sometimes, to be sure, the new assembly of the parts was somewhat unorthodox and bizarre (fig. 53); but the individual items, with some exceptions, were fairly authentic, and some were exact copies in wood of pierced screens from Ahmedabad mosques.

What had begun as a purely commercial venture had turned into a practical revival of a dying craft, and de Forest soon became a proselytizer. In 1885, he published a volume of photographs of the wooden and stone decorative carving on Indian houses of various dates, and placed with them views of his own apartments to show what such work looked like in an American home (fig. 53). In the introduction to the volume, he declared:

> It rests with us, both here and in Europe, to decide whether we are going to allow arts to die out which have taken centuries . . . to bring to perfection. There is but one way of saving them and that is, by giving employment to the best men in making the finest things. My work in this direction, which has been going on for more than four years, is no longer an experiment, and I can say with perfect confidence that better carving has never been made there, than I can have done at the present time.[87]

Not many responded to the call. The efforts of de Forest in Ahmedabad and Kipling in Lahore, like those of Hendley in Jaipur, provided some sustenance to craftsmen in those regions, but there was no sudden, widespread surge of interest. The survival of India's crafts remained a preoccupation of the Government's, but those crafts did not thereby achieve anything more than survival. The threats of extinction and adulteration of style were not lifted: the situation continued unchanged.

A measure of this lack of progress is provided by the exhibition of Indian art organized in Delhi under Government patronage by George Watt and Percy Brown in 1903. The exhibition brought together recent craft works in a broad range of categories including metalware, stoneware, glass, earthenware, woodwork, ivory carving, leatherwork, lacquer, textiles, embroidery, carpets, and fine arts. The organizers hoped to promote interest in these crafts, and to encourage the craftsmen to preserve their inherited traditions unchanged. Towards these ends, Watt made 'special efforts . . . to the exclusion of all trace of the modern foreign influences which have tended to debase the ancient indigenous arts of India'.[88] But had not all this been heard before? Were not these declared aims and methods precise repetitions of Hendley's in the Jaipur Exhibition twenty years before? In the intervening period nothing had changed. The general regeneration of India's crafts, so often hoped for, never happened.

The Government need not have been surprised by this, for what they sought

53. Mr De Forest's rooms, 9 East 17th Street, New York, from *Indian Domestic Architecture* (1885).

to achieve with one effort they deprived of all chance of success with another. The exhibition of 1903 was occasioned by the Delhi Durbar of that year, Curzon's celebration of the coronation of Edward VII. This was a magnificent pageant, a display of imperial power and civilization, which went on for a fortnight. The maharajas were of course invited, so that they might demonstrate their loyalty to the new Emperor, add colour to the occasion and be impressed by imperial splendour. Any interest in their own cultural heritage that might have been stimulated by a visit to the exhibition was likely to be swiftly erased by the other events on the programme. This particular method of claiming the maharajas' allegiance to Western culture, through claiming their allegiance to the Crown, had been initiated in the earlier Delhi Durbar, in 1877, when Victoria was declared Empress; it was repeated in the Delhi Durbars of 1911 and 1931, which celebrated the coronation of George V and the official opening of New Delhi. These events were the most spectacular and lavish displays of the might and style of the British Raj; it is scarcely any wonder that few maharajas returned from them to their native kingdoms and called for the *mistri*. The inconsistency of a government that sought to promote understanding and patronage of the Indian arts while creating conditions in which their traditional patrons would abandon them, ensured that the efforts of men such as de Forest and Kipling remained splendid but isolated, with no influence beyond their own duration.

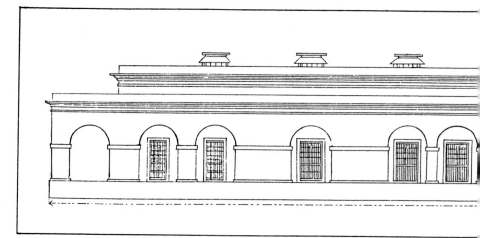

54. *Architecture as Understood by the Public Works Department:* elevation of the Bulandshahr District Court, published by J.L. Kipling in 1886.

## The Gathering Storm

Before they were curtailed by officialdom, Growse's efforts had briefly provided employment to the craftsmen of Bulandshahr, and although that success was limited and local, it acquired a wider significance by fuelling debate about the future of Indian architecture and Government responsibility in that future. Writers had been deploring the Westernization of Indian architecture and the decay of its traditions ever since Fergusson observed that colonial classicism had 'nearly obliterated all the native styles of India'.[89] Over time, the question assumed an increasing urgency, as the effects of Westernization seemed to become indelible and the chances of saving the Indian tradition faded. Growse's work gave the argument a new focus.

One of the first to cite Growse's projects as an example in this debate was Purdon Clarke, the Keeper of Indian Art at the South Kensington Museum. In a lecture read before the Royal Society of Arts in May 1884, while Growse was still in Bulandshahr, Clarke strongly commended his work, citing the Bulandshahr *chowk* as evidence of 'the latent power for true art work which exists in even the most unpromising of Indian towns'.[90] He defended Growse against the standard PWD charge that Indian design is expensive by recording that the development of the *chowk* was all achieved for £725. Later that year, when the first version of Growse's book on Bulandshahr appeared, it was warmly received by the press. *The Graphic*, for example, declared: 'Mr Growse cries out against the strangling effect of Government red tape, and also against the tyranny of the Public Works Department', and added, in a remark which must have made every Lieutenant Governor shudder, 'each district, in fact, wants a Growse to stir it up'.[91]

The next public defence of Growse came in 1886, after his transfer to Fatehpur, from John Lockwood Kipling in the newly founded *Journal of Indian Art*. The journal's second issue had been devoted to the industrial arts, in recognition

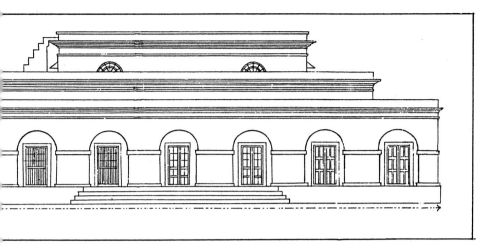

of the Jaipur Exhibition; the third opened with Kipling's article on Growse, which borrowed the title of Growse's polemic, *Indian Architecture of Today*. Kipling reflected on the changes in taste brought about by Government educational policies, noting that, 'with the classes stirred by English education, foreign styles stand for enlightenment and progress'.[92] As an example, he cited the gentleman of Bulandshahr whose choice of classicism as a style for his house (fig. 18) led him to quarrel with Growse. Kipling observed that, while it was understandable that such men should wish to imitate English styles, it was especially unfortunate that the particular examples of classicism that they most commonly encountered were the products of the PWD, and that they did not realize that these were the worst possible models. As an example of PWD work, Kipling published the elevation of Bulandshahr's District Court (fig. 54), and, following Growse's lead, he attacked the department's policies of standardization: 'There are hundreds of such buildings in India, where, cut up into longer or shorter lengths, they serve for law courts, schools, municipal halls, dak bungalows, barracks, post offices, and other needs of our high civilisation.' Again following Growse, he derided the department for refusing to employ the *mistri* except as a labourer: 'Year by year good men of the mistry class . . . grow rarer. They are scarcely to be found at all in the neighbourhood of our official centres, and when they are employed they are regarded as 'hands' merely by overseers who, in artistic sense, are their inferiors'.[93]

But Kipling went further than Growse in defending such men against the scepticism of the PWD. He pointed out that the department's lack of confidence in the *mistris* was partly due to their humble social status. They also tended to be illiterate; they were certainly not articulate self-apologists. More importantly, they worked according to their own distinct methods. The PWD accused the *mistris* of being haphazard in their work, but Kipling argued that they only appeared to be so: 'Their drawings are seldom to scale, perspectives are unknown, and the details are not carefully made out, for, as the mistry superintends the work himself, he does not think it necessary to elaborate on paper parts which will be better understood when they come to be worked *in situ*'.[94] It was assumed that, because the *mistri* did not produce finished drawings, he had no discipline. But an architectural drawing is no more than a set of instructions to a workman, and since, as Kipling observed, the *mistri* was his own workman, a few brief notes sufficed. This method might have been alien to the British engineer, but it had produced sound and well-conceived buildings in India for two thousand years before he arrived there.

Growse's work remained a potent example for defenders of Indian design to refer to even after the turn of the century. He was also cited by those whose interest lay in the decorative arts, as, for example, by J. L. Maffey, who referred to Growse in his pamphlet of 1903 on the demise of wood-carving in the United Provinces. Like many before him, Maffey observed how, with the Westernization of Indian taste, craft traditions were either stylistically debased or starved of patronage. He believed that educated Indians, noting the plainness of PWD structures, assumed that the plainness was aesthetically desirable (rather than simply economically expedient) and so forsook the richness of Indian carving: 'Thus, through being the object of the most sincere form of flattery, the English rule has caused the country to be sprinkled with plain, unlovely doorways and balconies, and has turned the *mistri* out of the verandah'.[95]

Maffey acknowledged that the Government was aware of the problem, and that it was doing much to increase the supply of authentic craft work, through exhibitions and the Schools of Art; but he accused it of doing nothing to increase the demand. He believed that what was required was a re-Indianization of the country's educated classes, for he supposed that ultimately the solution lay with them. He chided the maharajas for preferring Western artefacts, comparing them unfavourably with the Mughal Emperor Akbar, who had patronized local traditions.[96] Such commendation of Akbar was a platitude of the time,[97] but it did not occur to Maffey that the modern counterparts of Akbar were not the maharajas but the British Government; it was from the Government that the *mistri* required patronage, for few maharajas would revert to his services unless the Government set that example. Maffey did not perceive this, in spite of quoting Growse's demands for British patronage of the Indian arts, and consequently his version of the argument is a somewhat faint echo.

Soon, however, Growse's work and arguments fell into the hands of a polemicist even more ardent than himself. E. B. Havell was an art teacher and an art historian, and in both capacities was a forceful proponent of unorthodox views. As Superintendent of the School of Art in Calcutta between 1896 and 1905, he worked to reverse its Westernizing policies, encouraging the students to examine Indian art. In his writing, he vigorously (sometimes even incautiously) insisted on the originality of Indian art, disputing all theories of the foreign origin of its ideas. His *Indian Architecture* of 1913 contains sustained bursts of indignation and anger against many aspects of Western understanding of, and Government policy towards, Indian art. In its concluding chapters, he discussed the decline of the indigenous architectural tradition. Seeing, like Kipling and Maffey, the source of the problem in the education policy, Havell pinned the blame for the demise of Indian architecture on 'the arch-Philistine Macaulay – who was less fit to legislate for the education of Indian youth than a Brahmin pandit would be for the British public schoolboy', and he accused Macaulay of instigating a 'war of extermination against all the intellectual traditions of Hinduism'.[98] The frequent references to Macaulay are significant since, in a sense, Havell and the other critics of the PWD were fighting again the battle of the Orientalists against a Westernizing government.

Havell's objections to the PWD followed Growse's so far as he accused the department of abusing the *mistri* by offering him only labourer's work; but he added the further objection that the PWD abused architectural styles by treating them as interchangeable garments (and certainly some of the mongrels that the department produced (fig. 35) indicate a lack of regard to architectural grammar which would do credit to the architects of Lucknow). Havell described the usual PWD procedure:

> The official architect sits in his office at Simla, Calcutta, or Bombay, surrounded by pattern-books of styles – Renaissance, Gothic, Indo-Saracenic, and the like – and, having calculated precisely the dimensions and arrangements of a building suited to departmental requirements, offers for approval a choice of the 'styles' which please him or his superiors, for clothing the structure with architectural garments in varying degrees of smartness, according to the purpose for which it is intended, at so much per square foot.
>
> When these preliminaries are settled, a set of paper patterns is prepared and contractors are invited to undertake to get these patterns worked out to proper scale and in the regulation materials. Then, at last, the Indian craftsman is called in to assist in the operations, under the supervision of the contractor and subordinate Public Works officials, who check any tendency the craftsman may show to use his imagination or his intelligence in anything beyond copying the departmental paper patterns.[99]

Confronting the PWD allegation that the *mistri* was incompetent, Havell conceded that many *mistris* were indeed incapable of anything but the plodding execution of another's designs, but he argued that this was a direct result of PWD policy: allowed to do nothing but plodding work, the *mistri* became in time incapable of anything else, and then suffered the contempt of the PWD official who despised him for his carefully acquired incapacity and cited it as a reason for not giving him more responsible work. But, insisted Havell, there were other *mistris* yet untouched by the PWD, and these he urged the Government to employ: 'If we would all, dilettanti and experts alike, give up pretending to teach art, and, like Akbar, put ourselves to school, we should soon understand the true secret of Mogul architecture'.[100]

Against this assault of rhetoric and logic, the PWD remained unmoved. Growse and his supporters could demonstrate uncontestably that the PWD's specific fears regarding the quality and cost of the *mistri*'s work were groundless, but still they could not persuade the department to capitulate and employ him. This was because their arguments did not address the underlying, unstated objection: they could not wash out the distaste for Indian civilization felt by the generality of the British in India; they could not expunge the Macaulayite assumptions that India was essentially barbarous, that its traditions were worthless, and that British imperialism was civilizing. Given the general nature of those assumptions, similar conflicts could of course be found in a wide range of aspects of life in British India: in very many fields, a dispute arose between those who sought to hand responsibility to Indians and those who wished to retain it in colonial hands. Quite apart from the purely political sphere, such a dispute arose, for example, in the army: Jacob's Horse, the irregular unit of cavalry founded by Samuel Swinton Jacob's distant cousin John, was of the kind distinguished from standard units by having few British officers and relying on Indians to fill their place; John Jacob was among those who proposed this system for the whole Indian army, a policy of Indianization vehemently resisted by many, including another member of the family, General Sir Claud Jacob.[101] Just as the Westernizers won that dispute, so in architecture the British in India were prevented from adopting the patronage policies of Akbar by their deep-seated distrust of native traditions; they were not cultural pluralists as the Mughals had been, ready to place confidence in an alien system.

If, in the defence of that system, Havell was more shrill than his predecesors had been, this was because he wrote his book just after a decision had been taken, which would give the debate an entirely new significance. This decision made the crisis acute, because, as Havell perceived, it provided an opportunity of uncertain character: it could prove an opportunity to save Indian architecture at the final hour, but it could equally prove an opportunity finally to extinguish it. The urgency took the debate to a far wider audience; it was no longer a dispute between a few revivalists and the PWD but one which engaged large sections of the British public, Government and press. The decision, announced by the King himself in Delhi in 1911, was the transfer of the capital of British India from Calcutta to Delhi; the volatile opportunity arose from the consequent need to build an entire new city.

CHAPTER FOUR

# The Crossroads on Raisina

The audience at the Coronation Durbar on 12 December 1911 was already stunned by the display of imperial majesty when King George tersely announced the intended transfer of the seat of government from Calcutta to Delhi, without elaborating on the reasons. There were, in fact, several reasons. The move was primarily an attempt to escape the political atmosphere of Bengal, increasingly charged since the partition of that state by Lord Curzon in 1905. This political atmosphere greatly aggravated the climatic one, which had long been a source of dissatisfaction, as Calcutta's insufferable summer necessitated the removal of the entire administration to Simla for seven months each year. The transfer to Delhi did not solve this problem, but it eased it: Delhi's climate is marginally more bearable and so the retreat to Simla, though not obviated, could be reduced to five months; and the journey was shortened. A less dubious advantage of Delhi was the quality of its historical associations, for it had attached to it all the prestige of the early sultans and the Mughals. The Coronation Durbar was itself held in Delhi rather than in the capital so that the new King Emperor was installed into an older (if borrowed) pedigree; and the King reinforced the claim to the Mughals as ancestors when announcing the transfer by referring to Delhi as the 'ancient capital'.[1] Finally, the secrecy that shrouded the decision until the moment it was announced by the King, suggests that a significant part of its attraction was that it provided the opportunity for an announcement of great drama to mark the Durbar, and to distinguish it from its forerunners.

The King discussed none of these motives, and suggested instead that the transfer might be conducive to the greater happiness of the people, though instantly some of them began to wonder how. Voices of dissent were raised on both political and financial grounds: the residents of Calcutta, including the British residents, predictably objected loudest to their being turned into provincials; and Lord Curzon spearheaded those who regarded the exercise as disgracefully wasteful, accusing the Government of seriously underestimating the cost to the Indian taxpayer.[2] (Though Curzon was proved correct in that accusation, he was perhaps motivated by other considerations, for the transfer was accompanied by the reunification of Bengal and so drew attention to his earlier folly; and it was bound to distract attention from the Victoria Memorial Hall in Calcutta, which he had caused to be built and which he had intended to form the sanctum of the Empire.)

Of all the disputes that arose, the more lasting and productive were those that concerned the architectural character of the new city itself. There were two arguments on this subject, associated but properly discrete (though elided by some of those who took part in them, and consequently by some later commentators). The first concerned the choice of the architectual style for the new buildings, with some insisting that it must be Western, and probably classical, and others advocating that an Indian style or some shade of compromise be adopted. This argument was essentially a continuation of the nineteenth-century quest for a politically appropriate style, expressive of the imperial role. The second argument concerned method, for some (not E. B. Havell alone) proposed that the design and execution of the new buildings be entrusted wholly or predominantly to Indian *mistris* and to traditional Indian working practices; they perceived that the building of the city offered a magnificent chance, but probably the last chance, to rescue the Indian architectural guild system from extinction. Their proposal was more radical than a simple demand for the use of an Indian style, and, although occasionally confused with that demand, was distinct: it was a continuation not of the quest for an imperial style but of the arguments of F. S. Growse and the other revivalists.

The effects of these arguments about style and method were prejudiced by the appointment to the work on the new Delhi of two independently minded architects, Edwin Lutyens and Herbert Baker. However, their appointment was not immediate, but reached by degrees. In the first place, a town-planning committee was constituted and visited the site in the spring of 1912. The committee was led by George Swinton, the Chairman of the London County Council, and included also John Brodie, the municipal engineer of Liverpool. Lutyens was chosen from the many competitors for the post of architectural advisor to the committee, partly because of his experience in the planning of Hampstead Garden Suburb. It was not until the following spring that the architects who were to work on the buildings themselves were appointed. Again, many names were proposed, but Lutyens was carried over from the planning committee largely because of the considerable personal influence he exerted on the Viceroy and Vicerine, Lord and Lady Hardinge. Herbert Baker was appointed to be Lutyens's collaborator on Lutyens's own recommendation, substantiated by Baker's earlier achievements in Pretoria. As these two began to discuss the project and to draw up plans, there were still very many bystanders ready to advise them about how they should proceed with their designs.

*Selecting a Style*

In the matter of choosing an architectural style, the Indo-Saracenic, now fully developed, recommended itself for consideration. This style appealed especially to politicians, as it was seen by them to make an appropriate political gesture. Thus Lutyens was told that the Viceroy 'for high considerations of state felt bound to have an Indian styled city'.[3] At the outset, the Viceroy wanted the buildings to have a generally Indian appearance, in order to symbolize the increasing role of Indians in government; but mindful of the strong dislike for Indian traditions among the British in India, he proposed a compromise style which would include Indian motifs. This compromise or blend received support from other political figures including Lord Curzon (once he was adjusted to the idea that New Delhi should be built at all) and the Secretary of State for India, Lord Crewe. The King also broadly supported the use of Indian styles or features, and, in the House of Commons, a number of members, including Ramsay Macdonald, spoke in their favour.[4]

Accordingly, when Lutyens and Baker were appointed to design the buildings, Samuel Swinton Jacob – the acknowledged expert on Indian architectural details – was appointed as their advisor. Jacob was then seeing through the press the final part of his great *Jeypore Portfolio*, and his role in Delhi was to be what Lutyens called 'a sort of walking dictionary' of Indian architecture.[5] Although this appointment might have provided an opportunity for a revivalist to influence the design of New Delhi, in practice Jacob's involvement did not last long. He had by this time turned seventy and had recently returned to England to retire; although honoured, he was not overjoyed about being put back to work.

Indian styles found advocates not only among political figures but also among practitioners of Indo-Saracenic architecture, and notably in John Begg, the Consulting Architect to the Government of India, who had designed the Indo-Saracenic General Post Office in Bombay in 1909. Begg argued that the classicism of Calcutta was the style of 'mere Western occupation of the country', and that architectural policies should change with the political: 'Why should the style of our capital be such as to express most strongly those alien characteristics which every year tend more and more to disappear?' As Consulting Architect to the Government, Begg might reasonably have expected to be involved in the design of New Delhi; and, in advocating an Indo-Saracenic style, he was perhaps commending his own skills: there is something of a nudge in his observation that 'it is not impossible for the European architect to work in the spirit of this country. . . . There are some of us who have made the attempt, and are still persisting in it, not, I think, without success. . . .'[6]

As a political gesture, the use of an Indo-Saracenic style would have been (as ever) somewhat ironic, since the main thrust of British architectural policy in India had ensured that Indians were more likely to admire Western than Indian styles (though the critic Robert Byron claimed to have met one maharaja who supported the proposal[7]). Its opponents were those who wished to sustain that main thrust, for they also saw in New Delhi the opportunity to make a political gesture, but one of quite a different sort. An article in *The Builder* in 1912, for example, opened with the reflection that 'the greatness of a civilisation declares itself in its architecture' and the observation that, 'once having conquered the world, Alexander the Great controlled it not by the marshalling of troops, but by the founding and establishing of cities of Greek design.' As it pursued the relevance of this doubtful history lesson, the article nowhere referred directly to New Delhi, but its intended application was as clear as its message that it is the setting, not the following, of example which is the mark of the virile nation. It hinted that anything less than a wholly Westernizing architectural policy would threaten the very basis of the Empire, since 'when Great Britain is incapable of setting an example of architectural achievement to her dependencies other nations more virile will slowly but surely take advantage of her relapse.'[8]

George Birdwood, though renowned as a defender of India's crafts, similarly felt that when it came to building an imperial city – a record for posterity of the majesty of the Empire – something distinctively English was required. *The Times* came to the same conclusion by looking backwards in time: 'The building of it is part of the process to which we committed ourselves with Macaulay's famous minute on Education in 1835, and our architecture cannot be noble or even sincere unless it be the reflection of our own period and our own minds.'[9]

On the same page as that leading article was an article by Herbert Baker. Not yet appointed, and perhaps in a bold attempt to enhance his chances, Baker declared his own views on the subject. His premiss was that 'first and foremost it is the spirit of British sovereignty which must be imprisoned in its stone and bronze', and, thus, 'we naturally turn to the architecture of our public buildings in England while the Empire was in the making, the classic style of Jones and Wren and their followers in the eighteenth century.'[10] However, so as not unduly to upset any powerful proponents of Indian styles, he conceded that some Indian details might be inserted without disrupting the classical harmony.

Lutyens was less swift to capitulate on that point. He was appalled by the politicians' demands for the adoption of Indian styles, or for the insertion of Indian features. For one thing, he despised Indian architecture. Even before he had seen any examples of it, he pronounced Mughal architecture to be 'piffle'[11], and seeing it did not disturb that conviction. But the politicians were in earnest, and sent the members of the town-planning committee on study tours. In the spring of 1912, Lutyens and his colleagues were instructed by the Viceroy to examine the Mughal and Rajput buildings of Agra and Jaipur, and the following December they visited the early sultanate buildings of Dhar and Mandu. The view of Indian architecture that Lutyens formed on the strength of this field-work was not generally favourable. He subscribed to the long-popular theory that it owed its few beauties to Western influence, and he found nothing else to commend:

Veneered joinery in stone, concrete and marble on a gigantic scale there is lots of, but no real architecture. . . . Personally I do not believe there is *any* real Indian architecture or any great tradition. There are just spurts by various mushroom dynasties with as much intellect in them as any other art nouveau.

For Baker's amusement, he concocted recipes for Indian styles:

Hindu: Set square stones and build childwise, but, before you erect, carve every stone differently and independently, with lace patterns and terrifying shapes. On top, over trabeated pendentives, set – an onion.
Mogul: Build a vasty mass of rough concrete, elephant-wise, on a very simple rectangular-cum-octagon plan, dome in anyhow, cutting off square. Overlay with a veneer of stone patterns, like laying a vertical tile floor, and get Italians to help you. Inlay jewels and cornelians if you can afford it and rob someone if you can't. Then on top of the mass put three turnips in concrete and overlay with stone or marble as before. Be very careful not to bond anything in, and don't care a damn if it does all come to pieces.[12]

One has to admire the humour more than the perception. There are echoes of Macaulay in such passages: Lutyens's dismissal of India's architecture, like Macaulay's of her literature, was based on a slight acquaintance, and it contains the same mixture of ignorance, arrogance and wit. There are some indications that, with prolonged exposure, Lutyens learned to admire some individual Indian buildings, including the palace at Datia; but there is no sign of change in his general views.

As well as disliking Indian architecture in its original forms, Lutyens – being sensitive to matters of architectural grammar – deplored hybridization, and so abhorred Indo-Saracenic architecture as heartily as he did the original. Seeing Swinton Jacob as an exponent of the Indo-Saracenic style, Lutyens was irked by the imposition of his advice and an outspoken critic of his buildings, describing them as 'all made up of tit-bits culled from various buildings of various dates'.[13] He was wrong in general about Jacob (because he was ignorant of Jacob's sources and method), but the phrase is a fair analysis of much Indo-Saracenic architecture and shows how Lutyens despised its handling of tradition.

In his efforts to resist the proposals to Indianize New Delhi, Lutyens deployed his personal charms at the highest levels. According to his daughter, he successfully wooed the King away from an attachment to the Mughal style and, at one point, thought that he had converted even the Viceroy to 'a Western style – i.e. logic, and not the mad riot of the tom-tom'. However, the Viceroy continued to insist on the introduction of some Indian features, and advised Lutyens to use Islamic pointed arches. Exasperated by the shallowness of this political posturing and by the general failure to understand architectural logic, Lutyens declared: 'One cannot tinker with a round arch. God did not make the Eastern rainbow pointed to show His wide sympathies.'[14] But the political masters did not surrender; and as they prepared their designs, both architects had to make what they could of the instruction to integrate Indian forms.

## The Mistri in Delhi

Concurrent with the discussion about the choice of an appropriate style for New Delhi, was a further argument concerning the employment of Indian craftsmen. Many felt that Indian artists and master-masons should be involved in the design as well as the construction of the new buildings. Different people meant different things by this proposal. Some, perhaps, envisaged for the craftsmen a minor and supporting role, such as ensuring the accuracy of the Indian details. But others wanted all the design work to be left wholly or very substantially to the craftsmen; they saw in New Delhi the final chance to rescue the working methods and traditions of the guild system, slowly dying for lack of patronage, and they knew that the whole future course of architecture in India depended on the decision that was made. This idea was the product of no eccentric faction: if in the end it exerted less influence than the call for an Indian style, it gained considerable support and demanded serious attention.

The major irritant for the Government in the House of Commons was the Member for Somerset, Joseph King. Though his first questions on the subject of the new Delhi concerned the choice of style, King soon began to take up the cause of the Indian craftsmen. He wanted to know if the Government were aware of their existence, and whether such men would be considered for appointment to design the city's main buildings. He was repeatedly told that no decision about the appointment of architects or the selection of a style had been made. But as 1912 drew to a close, King began to suspect that the decision to appoint British architects who would work in a classical style had already been made secretly, and he was indignant: 'I want emphatically to protest against the revenues of India being made the servants of British or Italian art. I want the Indians to have a chance of working out the splendid craftsmanship and the splendid genius they possess.' The Financial Secretary to the War Office, who was responsible for deflecting King's frequent assaults, continued to tell him that no decisions had been taken.[15]

Another leading spokesman in the cause, of course, was Havell. The first edition of his *Indian Architecture* appeared in 1913; throughout this work, he defended craft traditions, for he aimed to focus public attention on that subject in relation to New Delhi. Though the book is ostensibly a work of architectural history, it has a polemical stance and absorbing preoccupation which Havell declared in its preface:

I have planned this work so as to make evident to expert and layman alike the relation between Indian architectural history and a great problem which is exercising the public mind at the present – the building of the new Delhi – and a question of much more vital importance – the preservation of Indian handicraft.

For fifty years Indian departmentalism has followed a system of building demoralising alike to the architect and the craftsman. . . What finer opportunity can there be than the building of the new Delhi for inaugurating a new architectural and educational policy which will remove the incubus . . .?[16]

In his concluding chapter, Havell pondered how the new city would be built:

If the old precedents are maintained, the cut of its official uniform – 'Renaissance', 'Indo-Saracenic', or whatever its name may be – will be decided by eminent European professors after grave deliberation; and when the fashion plates of the latest style have been duly admired by the British public, Indian craftsmen will be summoned from north and from south, from east and from west, as in days of old; but not to sit in durbar at the Padshah's Court – only to copy the eminent professors' paper patterns.[17]

At the end of his book, Havell published, as an appendix, a petition concerning the building of New Delhi, which had been presented to the Secretary of State for India in February 1913, just at the time when the final choice of architects was being decided. Though its rhetoric bears marks of Havell's hand, this petition was signed by one hundred and seventy-five people, including members of both Houses of Parliament (Joseph King among them) and leading figures in the arts such as Frank Brangwyn, Robert Bridges, Sydney Cockerell, A. K. Coomaraswamy, Thomas Hardy and George Bernard Shaw, as well as Havell himself. The petitioners made clear that they were not interested in the discussions about appropriate style:

They submit that the question to be discussed is, not in what style, but by what method the new city should be built; whether that of the modern architect in an office with his assistants, detached from materials, craftsmen, and site, carrying his buildings to completion upon paper, with pencil-trained mind and hands, and binding with details and specification those who are to build strictly within these limits; the method that has produced the public buildings of the nineteenth and twentieth centuries, and in India those of the Anglo-Indian cities: or, the method that has given us Westminster Abbey, Saint Sofia, Saint Peter's (Rome), and in India the Taj, the Palaces of Akbar and Shah Jahan, and the great public works of former times, that of the master-builder with his craftsmen, working in accustomed materials upon the site from simple instructions as to accommodation and arrangement such as would have been given to a master-mason or a master-carpenter by a medieval King who required a palace or a castle, or by a Bishop who desired to found a cathedral. This was the method that has produced all the great buildings of the world, and no modern buildings warrant the assumption that it can safely be departed from.[18]

From this argument, coupled with their claim that only in India did craft traditions still survive, it is clear that the petitioners wanted Indian craftsmen to be given a dominant, not a subsidiary, role in New Delhi. The case that medieval procedure was preferable to modern, was perhaps overstated and too generalized; and the Secretary of State might have been surprised by some of the evidence adduced (particularly the reference to St. Peter's). At any rate, the Government was not persuaded, and after a few months the petitioners received an answer just long enough to contain an ambiguity:

> The Government of India expresses the view that the particular method urged in the petition has in India, as elsewhere, long ceased to be applicable to works of any magnitude or of utilitarian purpose.
>
> They are, however, in full sympathy with the aims of the signatories, and it is their hope and intention that the work of the New Delhi should serve as an encouragement to the best craftsmen in India to seek employment on it, and should afford them an ample outlet for their traditional skill in the decorative arts.[19]

Soon after the petition had been presented, the campaign received a considerable impetus from the publication of an official report on Indian craftsmanship. This report had its origins in the period before the transfer of the capital was announced. In November 1910, the newly formed India Society, anxious to enhance public understanding of the Indian craftsman's work, proposed to the India Office that members of the Archaeological Survey of India should be instructed, when on tour, to examine modern Indian buildings to determine the present state of craftsmanship. The Government responded by commissioning one member of the Survey, Gordon Sanderson, to concentrate exclusively on such an investigation; and when the transfer of the capital was announced, instructed him to hasten his report because of 'the importance attaching to indigenous architecture in connection with the building of the new Capital of Delhi'.[20]

Sanderson's report fell short of answering the India Society's demands, as he himself acknowledged, because the lack of time obliged him to limit his enquiries to parts of northern India. But even in that limited area, he found ample evidence of the survival of strong local traditions, with some craftsmen still capable of producing high quality work at low cost. He therefore demonstrated that the campaigners' proposal was feasible. He illustrated his findings with over

55. Bhopal; Taj ul Masjid (c. 1911).

ninety photographs of new buildings in various towns in Rajasthan and north central India. Some of these specimens are weak in design – a weakness Sanderson attributed to Western influence – but many, including the vast Taj ul Masjid then under construction in Bhopal (fig. 55), he considered 'an eloquent testimony to the fact that the old Indian builders have not lost their skill'. Others, such as some recent houses in Bikaner (fig. 56), showed undiminished skills in detailing and carving. Sanderson drew up lists of the names of the best craftsmen in each of the cities he visited and documented their trifling rates of pay. The craftsmen were often amazed at an English official giving them so much attention, and Sanderson had some difficulty in this regard: some of them 'looked on me with suspicion and, thinking that I might be on some other quest, gave me wrong addresses'.[21]

Preceding Sanderson's accounts of his field-work was an introduction to the report by the Consulting Architect, John Begg. In parts of this, Begg showed some uncertainty about the feasibility of employing Indian craftsmen unaided; in spite of the evidence provided by his colleague, he encouraged the view that skilled *mistris* were few in number; and while he supported the policy of employing them in principle, he argued that, 'till we have a sufficiency of indigenous architects, there is no alternative but to be content with the substitute of European birth.'[22] This ambivalence was due less, perhaps, to any genuine apprehension than to Begg's continuing hope that the European substitutes might include himself; for elsewhere in his introduction, he drew somewhat different conclusions from Sanderson's report. He confidently declared that 'these photographs should amply prove to anyone who may have a doubt on the point the

111

56. *Moti Mal's House, Bikaner;* a plate from Gordon Sanderson's report (1913).

fact of the survival to the present day of a living tradition.' He called for a new architectural policy – one which would develop and modernize the indigenous tradition and give employment to its craftsmen – and suggested that it be in-augurated in the building of New Delhi.[23] Thus the recently expressed idea that Begg 'had little time for traditional Indian crafts' gives a somewhat partial account of his attitudes: though initially contemptuous, he became a significant enthusiast.[24]

Sanderson's and Begg's report gave a sharpened edge to King's questions in the House, as he cited it as evidence in his arguments. King sustained his assault throughout 1913, long after the appointment of Lutyens and Baker (which he protested against strongly), for he still hoped to secure for Indian craftsmen some important role. He suspected that the Government's assurances that Indian craftsmen would be given full scope to contribute to the decoration of the new city, would mean in practice their being given some minor or menial role. In July, he asked whether the Government of India

have decided that Indian craftsmen can only be employed as decorators in the building of the New Delhi; and, if so, whether the Secretary of State will advise the Government of India that this separation of the functions of

112

building and decoration, which does not obtain in Indian architectural practice, is calculated to be ruinous to Indian craftsmanship?

He was told, in traditional parliamentary fashion, that no such decision had been taken.[25]

The Sanderson and Begg report also helped Havell's petitioners to recover from the brusque rebuff delivered by the Secretary of State, and they soon returned to the fray. One of their number, A. Randall Wells, wrote a supplementary letter on their behalf. He observed closely the few phrases of the Secretary of State's reply; this led him first to indulge in a little sarcasm: 'I have to express on behalf of the signatories the great satisfaction with which they have learned that the Government of India is in full sympathy with their aims.' Then, having noted the Government's suggestion that Indian methods could not produce works of 'magnitude or of utilitarian purpose', he drew attention to the report which it had itself commissioned:

> At the time the petition was presented this report, the material for which seems to have been collected in 1911, was not available, but it entirely confirms the views expressed in the petition and illustrates them with some ninety plates, comprising examples of works of both magnitude and of utilitarian purpose . . . its evidence as to fact is unimpeachable, and any opinions expressed are those of the most expert advisers upon the subject that the Government can command. It is felt, that this being so, the views of the Government of India expressed in your letter must be those held before this report had been read, and that the signatories may hope for a further communication not only affirming the Indian Government's agreement with their aims, but acknowledging their realisation of the possibilities suggested.[26]

But the Government had already disowned Sanderson and Begg. Their report was published, as intended from the outset, by the Archaeological Survey – a Government department – but the volume was prefaced by a note declaring that 'the opinions expressed by Mr Begg and Mr Sanderson are personal to themselves and the Government of India is in no way committed to the approval of their views.'[27]

Events overtook the petitioners' campaign, for even as Wells composed their riposte, Lutyens and Baker were already at work. But the loss of the campaign with regard to New Delhi did not altogether extinguish the hope that Indian craftsmen would yet be rescued: a decade later, in 1923, the architect H. V. Lanchester brought the subject before the RIBA. Lanchester began by paying tribute to Havell; in then urging, once again, the employment of the *mistri*, he could no longer refer specifically to New Delhi, though he did still fell obliged to defend the *mistri* against all the stock criticisms and suspicions, which had not been put to rest in spite of the evidence accumulated against them.

The first of these suspicions was that there was no longer a living tradition

sufficiently strong on which to build. The contrary had been demonstrated repeatedly, by Jacob, by Growse, by Havell and by Sanderson. Lanchester could
only reiterate that the fear was groundless and that 'Havell is undoubtedly correct in his contention that the traditional art of the country still exists, and that
. . . it still possesses enough [vitality] to be worth cultivating by every means
available.'[28] The notion that the *mistri*'s method was shoddy and insufficiently
thought out (the objection that had been delicately hinted at in the Government's reply to the petition), Lanchester met with an argument borrowed from
Lockwood Kipling. The *mistri*'s method was not worse but merely different, he
suggested, and capable of equal or greater results. The work should be assessed
by those results, Lanchester pursued, but 'we have made the mistake of saying
that we do not care what the results are, provided the methods have been busi-
nesslike'. He could contradict the assumption that the *mistri*'s ornate work was
expensive from his own experience: 'I made inquiries as to the cost of such work
and found it less than we should have paid for the same thing. . . . Our obses-
sions are, therefore, not only destructive artistically but cannot even claim the
only merit that would excuse them, that of being cheap.'[29]

All of these arguments had been well rehearsed by the *mistri*'s various apologists in the preceding forty years. Most recently, in connection with the New
Delhi project, Havell, the petitioners, Sanderson and Begg had all indicated the
existence of craftsmen in India and stressed the quality and economy of their
work. They might as well have saved their breath. Sitting in Lanchester's
audience was Herbert Baker, who rose after the lecture to turn the discussion
towards the

> controversial question of the mistri . . . and as to how far they can be left
> in charge or in sole command of buildings. I think they could be so left in
> the case of simpler buildings of Indian character; but in that of larger and
> more highly organised buildings, such as are necessary for administrative
> and industrial development today, their primitive and charming methods
> are hardly suited.

The crushing condescension of that 'primitive and charming' reveals that Baker
had still not grasped the apologists' point regarding method. But Lanchester
was perhaps less exasperated by him than by another member of his audience,
Sir Lionel Jacob, who poured scorn on the Hindu tradition and denied the very
existence of the *mistri* (he cannot have read Sanderson's lists of names). One can
almost hear the gritted teeth in Lanchester's reply: 'Master mistries exist; I
showed you a photograph of one'.[30]

It will have been noticed that the arguments concerned only the existence,
competence and cost of the *mistri*; there was no suggestion that advocating his
employment indicated any disloyalty towards British imperial rule. Indeed, the
petitioners had been anxious to argue that their policy would 'tie the natives of
India more closely to the Mother Country', and although Begg spoke of a 're-

awakened India', he was evidently thinking of an India whose self-confidence flourished under British protection.[31] However much Havell challenged Government policies relating to architecture and education, he never questioned the value of British rule in general. If these men differed from their antagonists politically, it was because they saw the role of the Empire as paternalistic; they were guardians, not missionaries.

In 1927, as New Delhi approached completion, Havell produced a second edition of his book. In this, he could claim that the first edition had aroused discussion in Parliament and in the press, and he added a chapter censoriously entitled 'Fourteen Years After – An Imperial Object Lesson'. But in reviewing the development of the debate, in this chapter, Havell could do no more than repeat the same arguments again; there was little in the way of positive achievement of which he could boast.

Compared with the advocates of Indian styles, those campaigning on behalf of the *mistri* had made little headway with the Government. They had apparently aroused the interest of the King, though it is unclear how far his sympathy went. There was ample scope in this matter for ambiguity. One could declare an interest in the principle of employing *mistris* without indicating what role they were to have. And the question could be confused with that of style: that the Viceroy could speak of supporting the Indian tradition without for a moment contemplating any course other than employing an English architect, indicates that in some minds supporting the Indian tradition was equated merely with adopting an Indian style.

The petition was perhaps not entirely ineffective as, according to Baker, it was the spur that caused the Government to establish a school to train Indian craftsmen.[32] But the implication of this response – that the *mistris* needed to be re-trained before they were fit to work on New Delhi – shows that the Government had not accepted any part of the petition's argument, and the school was merely a conciliatory show of interest: in fact, a diversion. Accordingly, it was not taken seriously, and it was dropped during the War on grounds of cost. The accounts of Lutyens's wish to found a similar school may refer to a different project. His daughter has alleged that 'he longed to start a Delhi Centre for the training of Indian craftsmen for whom he had a great respect but he could get no Government cooperation for such a scheme.'[33] One might wonder what Lutyens proposed to teach Indians about craftsmanship. In the light of his views on Indian architecture, it is strange that he should have been interested in the craftsmen, unless of course he hoped, like the Government, to Westernize their methods. For one finds few examples of that respect – his more usual view was that no one in India knew 'any sort of craftsmanship except accountancy'.[34] The idea that Lutyens's proposal indicates a measure of agreement with Havell's views,[35] misses the point of Havell's argument, that the *mistri* did not stand in need of schooling from Englishmen (since his methods were already preferable), he merely needed employment.

When it came to the construction of the city, thousands of Indians worked on the new buildings, as labourers. Masons were brought from Agra, Mirzapur and Bharatpur; many claimed descent from those who had built the Mughal monuments, but they were not permitted to employ their inherited skills. For some lesser, decorative work, it was felt that Indians might be trusted, and an attempt was made to find Indian artists to help in the interiors; however, it was declared that none suitable could be found. Of course, the search for 'suitable' artists was a search for those capable of work sufficiently Westernized in style and technique to be applicable to Lutyens's and Baker's buildings. That none such could be found Havell called 'a decidedly scathing commentary on the Macaulay system of art education which has been followed in Government Schools of Art since they were founded.'[36] Lutyens employed Punjabi carpenters to execute his furniture designs, though he preferred to use Chinese, and he allowed neither to help in the design process. For Lutyens was not the sort of architect to tolerate collaborators: he designed every detail of Viceroy's House down to the doorhandles and the light fittings. Baker similarly employed craftsmen as executors, though he managed to summon some regret that it was 'impossible' to entrust them with more responsibility.[37]

That emphatic claim raises again the question whether the petitioners' proposal was practically feasible, whether the whole design could successfully have been entrusted to Indian *mistris* working in accordance with their traditional methods. Historical hindsight does not assist us in answering this question, for the evidence was available at the time, and the unsubstantiated assertion by some recent writers that the proposal was idealistic and impractical merely reiterates the fears and prejudices of that time. One of the first to review the question after the event was Lutyens's assistant, A. G. Shoosmith. Writing in 1938, Shoosmith acknowledged the force of those who had supported native building techniques, but he concluded that 'it is improbable that the work could ever have been completed by such methods'. A little later, the art historian Percy Brown (who had worked on the decoration of Viceroy's House) arrived at a similarly sceptical stance by misrepresenting the findings of Sanderson's report: the inquiry, he said, had revealed Indian artistic skills to be undiminished, 'but when the authority concerned came to inquire into the structural methods employed by the Indian builders it was clear that the same high quality of workmanship was not observable, his systems were primitive.'[38] In other words, Shoosmith and Brown followed the Government view that, though one might admire Indian artistry, one could not respect Indian technology (in spite of its past achievements) and so one could not employ the *mistri*. This attitude contrasts significantly with that which had been adopted by the British Government's predecessors on the imperial throne. The Mughals had similarly considered the Indian masons' methods to be primitive; sometimes (as at Fatehpur Sikri) they let this pass; at other times, they taught them new technologies (such as arcuate construction); but at all times, they continued to employ Indian masons as designers, in order to profit from the peculiar strengths of their tradition.

To regard the *mistri*'s primitive engineering systems as having been an insuperable obstacle misses the point of the apologists' argument. Such systems may indeed have been primitive, but they were also dispensable. It was not medieval engineering, but the co-operative method of designing and building which the advocates of the *mistri* saw as the essential factor to be retained. And it was possible to instruct *mistris* in modern engineering techniques while retaining this co-operative method. Swinton Jacob had already achieved this, broadening the repertoire of *mistris* without disrupting the traditional procedure of their work. So it was not idealistic to suppose that the procedure could be applied to large modern buildings: in fact, this too had already been achieved, not only by Jacob and his associates in such buildings as the Albert Hall and Lalgarh, but also (and more successfully perhaps) by Indian craftsmen working in Jacob's wake, on various public buildings in Jaipur and Bikaner, and by the craftsmen of some of the buildings illustrated in Sanderson's report. The idealism lay only in the supposition that the British Government might exercise the imagination characteristic of a Mughal one.

## Building the City

The debate about the *mistri* had involved many people and had generated much polemical writing, but it never for a moment jeopardized the employment of Lutyens and Baker. The story of the design and construction of New Delhi under the direction of these men, has been ably and thoroughly told, notably by Robert Grant Irving. The original division of labour gave Lutyens the responsibility for designing Viceroy's House (fig. 57) and Baker that for designing the two Secretariats. These buildings are grouped together on Raisina, a low hill standing to the south-west of the old Mughal walled city (fig. 58). Lutyens (according to Irving[39]) was also principally responsible for designing the street plan of the new city which sets the buildings in a complex, geometrical web. As the work progressed, certain political developments required further additions. The Montagu-Chelmsford Reforms of 1919 transferred power from a small Executive Council to a large Legislative Assembly and so created a need for an assembly building; Baker was accordingly asked to design the Council House, which stands slightly to the north of the main group. And following the War, Lutyens designed the All India War Memorial (or 'India Gate') to stand at the far end of King's Way, the axial road leading eastwards from Raisina (fig. 59). The Government was transferred to Delhi and put into temporary accommodation in April 1912; they remained there for a considerable period as the construction of the new buildings was delayed by the War, but at last New Delhi was formally opened with a Durbar in February 1931.

57. New Delhi;
Viceroy's House, by
Edwin Lutyens (1913-
31).

After all the controversy that had preceded and accompanied their design, the buildings could at last be assessed. In drawing up their designs, Lutyens and Baker responded differently to the demands made on them to introduce Indian features. Baker's aim remained that which he had expressed in his early article in *The Times*, namely, to interpolate into the classical tradition those Indian forms that jarred with it least; or, as he later expressed it, 'to weave into the fabric of the more elemental and universal forms of architecture the threads of such Indian traditional shapes and features as are compatible with the nature and use of the building' in the confident hope that such a weaving would symbolize a 'happy marriage' of political ideals.[40] As already remarked, Lutyens was more reluctant to tamper with tradition. Constrained by his employers to take some notice of the Indian heritage, he decided to attempt a more profound kind of union. As he told Valentine Chirol,

> To express modern India in stone, to represent her amazing sense of the
> supernatural, with its complement of profound fatalism, is no easy task.
> This cannot be done by the almost sterile stability of the English classical

118

58. New Delhi; the Government buildings seen from the east, with the Secretariats to left and right and Viceroy's House beyond.

59. New Delhi; the All India War Memorial, by Edwin Lutyens (1919-31).

119

61. New Delhi; details of a *chattri* by Herbert Baker.

60 (facing page). New Delhi; detail of the northern Secretariat, by Herbert Baker (1913-31).

style; nor can it be done by capturing Indian details and inserting their features, like hanging pictures on a wall! In giving India some new sense of architectural construction, adapted to her crafts, lies the great chance of creating what may become a new and inspiring period in the history of her art. . . . By this you will see where I am fearful of a Viceroy's arbitrary insistence on features and insertions.[41]

In spite of their different aims, Lutyens and Baker achieved similar results. Both began with classicism, since to both the classical tradition embodied order and rationalism, and thus could symbolize the Empire which itself was taken to embody those qualities: Baker, for example, sought to express by it a 'conception of orderly government'.[42] Onto the classical frame, both then grafted a selection of Indian forms: the *chajja*, or dripstone; the *chattri*, or domed kiosk; the *jali*, or pierced screen; corbelled arches; and sculptures of elephants and of bells on chains (figs. 60-61). Although a classical structure has been substituted for a Gothic one, this mixture continues the basic formula of certain Indo-Saracenic buildings: forty years earlier, architects such as F. W. Stevens had similarly grafted Indian motifs onto Gothic buildings (fig. 22).[43]

This sort of mixture was, of course, exactly what Baker claimed to be aiming

62. New Delhi; the northern Secretariat, seen from the west.

at, and critics have generally credited him with achieving nothing more. One of the earliest critics of New Delhi, Robert Byron, was especially emphatic on this point, describing Baker's use of Indian motifs as mere 'allusion' and 'writing in symbols'; he mocked Baker's frequent use of *jalis*, comparing them to 'the open-work stockings of Edwardian actresses'.[44]

Lutyens, by his own account, was attempting something deeper, and he has generally been credited with having achieved it: with having achieved, in fact, nothing less than the long sought-after synthesis or fusion of Eastern and Western traditions, that elusive goal which had tantalized architects in India for a century. Byron and Lutyens's follower A. G. Shoosmith both described Lutyens's work in such terms, and recent writers have followed their cue.[45] It is difficult to see how this description might be attested by reference to the buildings themselves. It is certainly true that Lutyens deplored the idea of simply interpolating Indian forms, and he thought little of Baker's work, but for the most part his own was similar in practice. Lutyens far surpassed his colleague in inventive genius, and accordingly he altered and adapted the Indian forms to a greater degree, but still he used them as punctuation marks, as occasional pauses in the classical scheme. The sprinkling of a few simplified and classicized Indian details (especially *chattris*) over a classical palace cannot be called a 'synthesis' or 'fusion' if those terms are to indicate more than interpolation. The so-called Delhi Order which Lutyens created at Viceroy's House consists of model bells and a stylised Asokan capital placed over a stripped classical column: this is not synthesis but combination. Above all in their logic and grammar, Lutyens's buildings are entirely classical (and superb examples of that tradition): nothing of their planning and massing, their proportions and relations of parts, or the

122

density and rhythms of their ornament, owes anything to any Indian precedent. Consequently, the Indian contribution consists only of inserted details.

At the outset, Lutyens had resisted the insertion of Indian features on the ground that the mixing of traditions would mock them; but since he was unable to integrate them as fully as he hoped, the result is just what he deplored. Placed over the classical colonnades of Viceroy's House, the *chajja*, for example, loses its original sense and becomes arbitrary. It is pressed into service as a cornice, and so becomes the logical complement to the cornice on the Kaisarbagh gate in Lucknow which was pressed into service as a *chajja* (fig. 6). The difference is that while the Lucknow form is clumsy, Lutyens's is supremely graceful, but it is no more of a fusion.

The single exception to this, the one part of the work in which Lutyens did achieve a kind of synthesis, is the dome of Viceroy's House (fig. 57). As is often remarked, the outline of the dome and the modelling of the drum are reminiscent of the tumulus and railings of the early Buddhist stupa at Sanchi, but it is not through any clumsy archaeological reference that the synthesis is achieved. Rather, Lutyens perceived in the Buddhist monument, a symbol of order and an elemental geometry fundamentally in harmony with the principles of classicism, and it is on that common spirit that he drew. He did not mix details, but produced an original form that is at the same time wholly classical and wholly Buddhist in spirit. It is a form which has shed individual reference, a form of awesome power and impartiality. It is architecture of unfettered intellect, calmly attesting to the humanistic principles shared by the disparate traditions from which it has arisen.

That, with the exception of this dome, Lutyens's buildings are not everything that he aimed for (and not what critics have called them) need not obscure their remarkable merits. Throughout Viceroy's House, each architectural vista – each view down a corridor, up a staircase, or into a distant hall – has been calculated with consummate mastery; and the detailing – of doorways and cornices, for example – is always eloquent and inventive. Even the scattered *chattris* are powerful, sculptural forms; and their qualities are translated to a larger scale in the War Memorial (fig. 59). Baker's Secretariats, too, have a sculptural power: although the towers at their eastern ends are somewhat gauche, there is a dynamic rhythm to the grouping of the columned projections on their inner flanks (fig. 62), so that they form a picturesque foil to the more reticent solemnity of the east front of Viceroy's House, which they frame.

The major weaknesses of the group of buildings concern the larger aspects of their planning. Baker's Council House, uncomfortably appended to the previously resolved scheme, stands on no significant axis and is too obviously an afterthought. A more serious planning fault, often commented on,[46] arose from Baker's insistence that the Secretariats should share the summit of Raisina, which was originally to be reserved for Viceroy's House alone. Baker's rationale characteristically involved political symbolism: he argued that the bureaucracy should be seen to be an equal, not an inferior, part of government. In consequence, to make space for the Secretariats, Viceroy's House was pushed back from the crest of the hill and so, although it is visible from a distance and from the summit, it is invisible to anyone standing at the foot of the hill, in the Great Place, because it is obscured by the hill itself. Indeed, as one moves along King's Way towards the buildings, Viceroy's House appears to sink into the ground as one's angle of view steepens (fig. 58). Lutyens called this effect his 'Bakerloo', and agitated to have it nullified by a cutting away of the crest of the hill. He noticed the mistake too late, however, for anyone to take his rectifying proposals seriously, and it stands as a serious flaw in the whole conception.

The street plan of the city is not successful either. It is a confusing web of triangles stacked in hexagons with a roundabout at each junction. Its debt to the Garden City makes it less of a city than a giant cantonment. Its bungalows stand isolated on large plots, and its streets are empty of people and urban vitality. Even after sixty years (and a considerable growth in the population), parts of it retain a suburban tranquillity: at night, dogs come out of houses to sleep in the streets where they are guaranteed undisturbed peace. King's Way (now Rajpath) was always purely ceremonial, for it leads nowhere that anyone wants to go, and except during Republic Day parades, it is lifeless.

But the potency of New Delhi lay not in any aspect of its planning so much as in the modern classicism of Lutyens's buildings. Lutyens had brought to India a new idiom which was to leave its mark on subsequent architecture there.

## The Legacy

In Lutyens's letter to Valentine Chirol, quoted above, there is a hint that he hoped to foster a new movement in Indian architecture. Initially, imitation of his work was restricted to a group of English architects working in his circle. Lutyens himself had shown how his modern classical style (with or without Indian flourishes) could be applied to smaller, less ceremonial buildings, for in addition to the major projects described, he also designed the National Archives building, and two town houses for Indian rulers, Baroda House and Hyderabad House.

In the course of the 1930s, a number of architects followed that example. Robert Tor Russell succeeded Begg as the Consulting Architect and was kept busy designing very many buildings in the new capital. He turned out designs for bungalows, post offices, police stations, the shops of Connaught Place and the East and West Court buildings, mostly in the customary, pedestrian, PWD manner; but the inspiration of Lutyens raised him to a higher plane when he designed the residence of the Commander-in-Chief. He was succeeded in 1939 by Henry Medd, who had already produced Delhi's two cathedrals in a style influenced by Lutyens and was then at work on the High Court of Nagpur, for which he frankly copied the dome of Viceroy's House. Shoosmith was also in-

fluenced by Lutyens when designing the Lady Hardinge Serai and St. Martin's
Garrison Church, both in Delhi.[47] In this last, famously bizarre, building, he developed not only the modern classicism of Lutyens's style, but even more its
powerful plasticity. Because this quality is also essential to traditional Hindu
temple architecture, Shoosmith (perhaps fortuitously) came closer than his
teacher to assimilating Indian architectural values. But the main importance of
all these buildings by Lutyens's followers – in the context of the present analysis
– is that they served to amplify the master's voice, and to demonstrate how it
might be imitated.

    After the country acquired independence in 1947, the architectural field was
left entirely to Indians. The new leaders of independent India did not immediately turn to the rescue of the *mistri*. This may have been due to their own
Westernized tastes, but in all probability it was already too late for such a rescue.
Sanderson's report had shown that, in 1913, the basis for a revival of the guild
system still existed, but that it needed the impetus of major employment; the
construction of New Delhi had offered the last such opportunity, but in the
event it had instead reinforced the use of Western building methods. By 1947,
the Indian craft tradition had probably already been starved to death; certainly,

63. New Delhi; the
Supreme Court, by
architects of the central
PWD (c. 1955).

125

the employment of the *mistri* has not since been contemplated in any major Indian architectural project.

The British PWD had always employed those Indian masons who were willing to retrain in the engineering schools and adopt PWD working procedures. Such men now filled the upper ranks of the PWD and, in an example of that bureaucratic continuity which frequently accompanies political upheaval, set about producing the public buildings of independent India in the manner of long-established colonial practice. An early example of their work is the Supreme Court in Delhi (fig. 63). This is a utilitarian structure crowned with a risible echo of Lutyens's great dome, and supplied with a red sandstone basement also copied from Viceroy's House. Later Ministry buildings (flanking Rajpath) debase the style yet further by removing any dignity of proportions still remaining and placing weak imitations of Lutyens's classicized *chattris* on vast and graceless blocks. Baker had expressed the determination that 'in 2,000 years there must be an Imperial Lutyens tradition in Indian architecture'.[48] It has not, in fact, lasted as long as that, but since British rule supplied Indian architects not only with the style of Lutyens but also with the working habits of the PWD, that is not to be lamented.

Considered in themselves, the buildings by Lutyens and Baker in New Delhi – and especially Viceroy's House – are magnificent achievements of architectural design. But they marked the final demise of India's indigenous tradition, and, as Havell reflected, 'New Delhi might have been something better than an excellent one-man show'.[49] As the Government's refusal to employ Indian craftsmen in design ensured the extinction of the guild system, so the architects' introduction of a new and potent idiom severed subsequent Indian architects from their own heritage. Had the Government adopted the policy of their Mughal predecessors and entrusted the designing of the buildings to Indian craftsmen, after schooling them only in modern engineering, the results might have been less dramatic and successful than the buildings that now stand, but one of the world's most distinctive architectural traditions would at least have been sustained a little longer, and might even have been given a new direction. Then, perhaps, something of the 'new and inspiring period in her art' of which Lutyens spoke might indeed have been achieved. It was for some such 'real co-operation' leading to 'a new lease of life' that Havell had hoped.[50] From this point onwards, the Indian architect had nothing of his own traditions to work from, but only what the West had given him. In the immediate future, as already shown, this meant the Lutyens idiom and the procedure of the PWD, and led to buildings such as the Supreme Court. But the future held many more gifts, for Western influence did not cease with the British Raj.[51]

# CHAPTER FIVE

# Independence and Dependence

Through the foregoing account of the major developments in Indian architecture in the colonial period, run certain recurring themes. These include: the adoption by Indian architects of the architectural vocabularies that were employed by Western architects in their buildings on Indian soil; changes in taste and patronage among India's educated classes, and the power of Western opinion on those changes; attempts at fusions of Eastern and Western traditions, or at revivals (real or sham); uses and abuses of tradition; and comments by Western critics. In spite of the clean political break and the abrupt introduction into India of the modern international style, the major developments in Indian architecture since 1947 all have their origins in the colonial period; and in the following brief survey of the later period the themes will be the same. This survey makes no claim to be a complete account of Indian architecture since 1947; it is a sketch of influential episodes and dominant preoccupations.

## Le Corbusier in India

According to A. G. Shoosmith, the influence of Lutyens had been overtaken even before Independence, by other influences from continental Europe; and he lamented how 'degenerate native architecture lies suffocated under a heaped chaos of foreign importations'.[1] Independence provided more opportunities for such importations, and one in particular, which was decisive. With Independence came Partition, and the price that India paid included the glittering city of Lahore, contained in the portion of Punjab that went to Pakistan. In an effort at compensation, the new central government provided the rump of Punjab with a new city to serve as its capital, Chandigarh. India's Prime Minister, Jawaharlal Nehru, attached great significance to this new city; seeing it as a symbol of the new India, he wanted it to be something distinctively modern, something which would look ahead into the country's future. India was in a mood to forget the past. The irony was that, to Nehru, as to most of India's ruling elite, modernism meant Westernism; they turned to the West to find the forms of modern architecture, and so the determination to look to the future, in practice con-

64. Chandigarh; the High Court, by Le Corbusier (1951-55).

tinued the patterns of that recent past that they most wished to escape. The choice of architect fell naturally on one of the founding fathers of the West's Modern Movement, Le Corbusier.

A team including Pierre Jeanneret, Jane Drew and Maxwell Fry assisted Le Corbusier in the construction of Chandigarh between 1951 and 1964, though the city plan and administrative buildings were chiefly his own conception. The plan has not generally been rated a success because of its lack of relation to the social realities of Indian urban life.[2] The spacious grid of wide streets is more elegant than the tight convolutions of a traditional town, but the traditional pattern had developed in response to actual living habits and needs, such as the use of the street as a market and meeting place, and the need for shade. Le Corbusier perhaps expected those habits and needs to undergo some dramatic change in the modern era; certainly, he designed for a society that did not then exist (and does not yet). When he did respond to local conditions, he did so clumsily: from the scale and width of Chandigarh's streets, it is often supposed that the city was designed for the motor car, though few of its inhabitants were likely to possess one; but, we are told, Le Corbusier was well aware that most Indians walk

128

65. Chandigarh; the Secretariat and (foreground) part of the Palace of Assembly, by Le Corbusier (1951-58, 1951-62).

rather than drive, and so deliberately devised a plan that would give the residents ample opportunity to walk.[3] As in the residential portions of Lutyens's New Delhi, the low density of the city also deprives it of a sense of place.

Le Corbusier was responsible in addition for the design of the buildings of the city's Capitol: the High Court (fig. 64), the Secretariat, and the Palace of Assembly (which houses the State's Legislative Assembly) (fig. 65). His design for the Governor's Palace, which was to complete the group, has not been executed. His work in Chandigarh is thus comparable in function and in quantity to that undertaken by Lutyens and Baker together in New Delhi, though it is not the whole of his work in India. The wealthy and Westernized textile industrialists of Ahmedabad took advantage of the presence in India of a progressive Western architect and invited him to their own city. In democratic, independent India, such industrialists displaced the maharajas as the patrons of new architectural fashions. Le Corbusier designed in Ahmedabad the Millowners' Association building (completed in 1954) (fig. 66), a Cultural Centre (completed in 1958) and three private houses (though one of these was abandoned in construction).

129

66. Ahmedabad; the
Millowners' Association
building, by
Le Corbusier (1951-54).

Le Corbusier was required by his clients – and most explicitly by Nehru – to give India a new architecture, 'unfettered by the traditions of the past'.[4] This is just what he delivered. Compared with anything that had then been built in India, his designs at Chandigarh and Ahmedabad were startlingly and uncompromisingly modern. That Le Corbusier broke with India's cultural traditions even more rudely than the imperialist Lutyens had done, is to some, perhaps, a dismaying thought, and recently it has been argued that his buildings are not entirely unfettered by tradition, that certain elements of their visual language were inspired by India's architectural heritage.

William Curtis has been the main proponent of this sentimental theory, insisting that Le Corbusier's aim was to 'acknowledge India's magnificent spiritual and built traditions but without lapsing into a spurious Orientalism or else pastiche'.[5] Curtis suggested that the Governor's Palace at Chandigarh, 'silhouetted against the sky, at the end of a vista of platforms, terraces and pools, recaptures the stance of the Diwan-i-Khas at Fatehpur Sikri'. This, his most convincing example, is at best a vague reference and occurs in the part of the project not built. The alleged references to Indian tradition in the existing buildings are weaker. For example, Curtis suggested that the *brise-soleil* shade, used so liberally by Le Corbusier, is a resonance of the traditional Indian hypostyle hall; others might think that, although certainly a response to the same problem of climate, it is a different and foreign response. Curtis saw, in the long and low

130

profile of the High Court (fig. 64), the outline of a Mughal *diwan-i-am* (audience hall); though one might with equal justification see the outline of a Greek temple. Similarly, he related the Millowners' Association building in Ahmedabad (fig. 66) to the fifteenth-century tomb complex at nearby Sarkhej, on the ground that both have columns and afford a view over water – a slight relation, involving commonplace features. He was on firmer ground in asserting that the funnel on the roof of the Palace of Assembly was inspired by the cooling towers of a power station outside Ahmedabad, for Le Corbusier is known to have admired them; but while they are undeniably striking forms, they are not part of a uniquely Indian tradition. Finally, Curtis suggested that the Capitol at Chandigarh is reminiscent of an ancient temple complex, because 'the naked concrete gives to the buildings an ancient patina as if they had been standing there for centuries';[6] perhaps, after all, Curtis intended self-parody, but some might feel that the use of a material so unsuited to the climate that it appears shabby within thirty years of construction, displays not so much respect for tradition as unconcern for reality.

Curtis's theory has found some measure of acceptance, though other commentators have seen in Le Corbusier's work in India little or no reference to Indian antecedents, and suggest that it is better understood in the context of his own œuvre than that of any specifically Indian development.[7] The little evidence afforded by Le Corbusier himself concerning his intentions in this regard is contradictory. In a letter to his colleagues at the start of the project, he expressed a wish – reminiscent of one of Lutyens's – to create 'a fundamental organic architecture, unquestionable, which is neither English, nor French, nor American but Indian of the second half of the twentieth century'. But in the same letter, he implied that something ready-made might do: 'India hasn't yet created an architecture for modern civilization (offices, factory buildings). India jumps suddenly into the second era of mechanization . . . we will be able to fulfil our mission: to give India the architecture of modern times'.[8] His buildings in India, like all his designs, incorporate some powerful, sculptural shapes. Some observers see in these shapes reflections of objects that are known to have caught Le Corbusier's eye when he visited India: the horns of cattle, astronomical instruments, and baskets carried on heads.[9] These objects may indeed have been his sources; but even if they were, their reflections do not of course constitute references to India's traditional architecture.

Though Le Corbusier's link with India's architectural past was at best tenuous, the future was firmly in his grip. The Modern Movement was not unheard of before he went there, but the production of buildings on Indian soil by one of its leading exponents had a profound effect. The architects of India were by this time, as remarked above, a new breed; they were not *mistris* but designers trained in Western procedures, lacking the *mistri*'s inherited repertoire of style. Le Corbusier provided these architects with a new vocabulary of forms, a new aesthetic. Many architects now practising in India have acknowledged Le Cor-

67. New Delhi; Akbar Hotel, by Shiv Nath Prasad (1965-69).

busier's importance in the propagation of modern architecture in the country,[10] for his work was quickly followed by large numbers of imitations.

Sometimes the new imagery was a little undigested, as in the Akbar Hotel (1965-69) (fig. 67), and the Sri Ram Centre (1966-72), both designed by Shiv Nath Prasad in New Delhi. Other buildings show a more considered response. In early projects by B. V. Doshi, who worked with Le Corbusier personally – such as the Tagore Hall and the Institute of Indology, both in Ahmedabad (figs. 68, 69) – the influence of Le Corbusier is still potent. But though Doshi himself has said that such designs were produced 'when I was filled with Le Corbusier',[11] there are traces of a more generalized influence of Modernism.

For, Le Corbusier, as well as giving Indian architects his own imagery, directed attention to the larger store of the modern West. This process was re-peated a decade later, when Louis Kahn was commissioned to design the Indian Institute of Management in Ahmedabad (1962-72) (fig. 70). (With buildings by Le Corbusier, Doshi and Kahn, Ahmedabad is a major centre of the country's modern architecture of the 1950s and '60s; it is also the home of one of the country's leading schools of architecture.) Curtis, of course, has argued that Kahn's design was influenced by the Indian tradition,[12] but though it includes some echoes of Mughal organization and colour schemes, its most impressive feature – its vast, abstract geometrical shapes – introduced a strange and won-derful visual language.

The influence of the Modern Movement in India soon became such a strong tide that it drowned altogether the voices that continued to urge the retention of Indian values and forms. There were still a few such voices, including that of

132

68. Ahmedabad; Tagore Hall, by B.V. Doshi (1960s).

69. Ahmedabad; Institute of Indology, by B.V. Doshi (1962).

70. Ahmedabad; Indian Institute of Management, by Louis Kahn (1962–72).

Claude Batley. Before Independence, in 1934, Batley had published a volume of measured drawings of details of traditional Indian buildings. Though on a much smaller scale, the project bore some resemblance to Swinton Jacob's *Jeypore Portfolio*, and it arose from the same motives: the range of examples illustrated was wide but, as Batley explained, it concentrated on 'smaller domestic architecture, from which, perhaps, the most useful inspiration may be gleaned by architects in connection with their practice in the India of today'.[13] Later, observing the power of the Modern Movement, Batley complained, 'it is pathetic that India's youngest generation of architects should be so infected with an inferiority complex . . . as to prefer to take their cue from the hastily developed, inadequately tested but ready to hand ideas of the West . . .'. Batley looked to this young generation to build a new Indian architecture 'on the solid base of their own tradition as eminently suited by long usage and experiment to the India of the future'.[14]

He was not entirely alone. In 1956, the architect B. L. Dhama, who had worked in the Archaeological Survey, also produced a book of traditional architectural details, 'in order that it might, perhaps, prove useful to the people engaged in architectural and engineering activities and other allied arts at the moment when the old architectural and educational policy is engaging the attention both of the Government and the public'. Dhama's hope was that students would be inspired by these details, not that they would copy them; he hoped that they would thereby 'introduce an entirely new style of architecture to suit modern conditions in which the Indian genius may not be lost sight of'.[15]

The proposals of Batley and Dhama echoed those of Jacob, but they met with less success. The few architects who were attempting to follow such a policy were not *mistris*, schooled in the Indian tradition since birth. They were architects who studied the indigenous sources as outsiders, and who had also before them the interpretations of those sources made by earlier generations of outsiders – the work of the Indo-Saracenic architects and Lutyens and Baker. Their products include the Vidhana Soudha, the Legislative Assembly built by architects of the Karnataka State Public Works Department (1952-57) and the Supreme Court in Delhi, already described (fig. 63). Such exercises were never successful, and the influence of the Modern Movement ensured that they did not continue after the 1950s.

That influence therefore completed the process of extermination and change that had begun over a century before. The influence of colonial architecture had disrupted traditional design. British imperial policies regarding education and architecture had further damaged traditional design by altering taste among patrons. Attempts at a craft revival in the late nineteenth century had produced some fine buildings but had not proved enduring. The work of Lutyens and Baker had finally extinguished the procedural traditions of Indian architecture; it had also introduced a new stylistic idiom and thus severed the new breed of Indian architects from their heritage, which they were able to see only through Western eyes and reproduce only in imitations of Anglo-Indian imperial styles. Finally, Le Corbusier and the Modern Movement more generally, severed Indian architects even from that vestigial Indian identity, replacing it with a wholly alien, international style. The last of these episodes took place in an independent India, but there was scarcely an element of free choice in it:[16] a century and a half of the imposition of Western architecture and the destruction of native traditions had left Indians with nothing of their own, so that they had little choice but to continue taking what the West had to give, whatever that might be.

The nadir of this unhappy history has now been reached; the prophecy reiterated by polemicists from Fergusson to Havell was fulfilled: distinctively Indian architecture was apparently extinct, its traditions had disappeared.

## The Indian Identity

In 1942, the art historian Percy Brown predicted that, with the introduction into India of concrete, 'there will be a tendency to subordinate individuality and nationality, so that all buildings will be of a standardized pattern'.[17] As soon as it was realized that the distinctly Indian identity had indeed been lost, some Indian architects began to question whether this was not to be regretted, whether that identity might not be retrieved. They did not wish to return to the historicism of the last century, nor to any kind of craft revivalism, and they did not wish to jettison everything that had been learned from the West; yet still they wanted their own, independent voice. It occurred to them that they might attempt to combine the advantages of the Modern Movement with some aspects of the Indian tradition, while still looking forward. One of the principal figures in this movement, Charles Correa, has spoken of 'the necessity to simultaneously both rediscover India's past and invent its future';[18] and another, Raj Rewal, has explained: 'Our generation has been trying to discover the common thread with which the fabric of Indian architecture has been woven in the past and its significance for our times'.[19] They have thus joined the long list of those who have gone in quest of a fusion of East and West, in this case a fusion of the Modern Movement with elements of a revived Indian idiom. Their efforts began as early as the 1960s, but were at first tentative and occasional; they have been in earnest only in the present decade. In their various projects produced so far, the degrees of commitment and success vary.

Their work may be seen as a part of a more widespread dissatisfaction with the legacy of the Modern Movement: the International Style tended to crush regional identity throughout the world, and the Indian movement is one of many local forces, attempting to re-establish such identity. The various regional movements are further analogous, as a form of dissent, to the Post-Modernists' attempt to undo the destruction of tradition. But although the Indian movement can therefore be related to foreign developments, and although some measure of discontinuity in the wake of Modernism has been experienced everywhere, still a regional movement by its very nature is concerned with local not international issues, and the particular architectural history of India gives it a unique focus.

The sometimes frenzied search for the lost Indian identity is reflected in the titles of a number of recent articles by practising architects: Raj Rewal has written on 'The Relevance of Tradition in Indian Architecture', and Ram Sharma on 'The Search for Roots and Relevance'.[20] But the frequent recurrence of the word 'relevance' indicates another preoccupation. The architects of this movement are alert to the hazards of pastiche; they have made a conscious determination not to regard the architectural heritage as a store of traditional motifs which can be attached to modern buildings to Indianize them. They are insistent that tradition must be interpreted; it must be integrated with, not sprinkled over, Modernism. Thus Charles Correa contrasts 'transfers' (the literal quotation of historical forms) with 'transformations' (the assimilation of them), and he has a horror of 'grave-digging'.[21] Another architect, of a slightly younger generation, Uttam Jain, is equally emphatic: 'My dependence on Indian traditional architecture is derivative rather than imitative. It is a response to culture, climate, people, materials, historical spaces and not to literal built forms. . . . Pastiche has no room in my belief'.[22]

Malay Chatterjee suggests that this concern arises from a political self-consciousness. Chatterjee argues that, before Independence, to many people the question of style was the question of how much Indianization to allow without appearing to make political concessions to the subject people. But, 'after Independence, the question changed to: How much indigenisation could a newly independent nation afford without appearing backward and weak both in its own eyes and in the image it presented to the rest of the world?'[23] This is no doubt true, but it is clear that the concern arises also from genuine misgivings about the abuse of tradition. These misgivings are quite reasonable, and India is full of nineteenth-century buildings that might engender them.[24] The experiments by Indian architects with the Western classical tradition at Lucknow and elsewhere, and those by British architects with Indian traditions (in Indo-Saracenic buildings and in New Delhi) all demonstrate the pitfalls of using traditional forms as emblems, attaching them to buildings of a basically different character, in the hope of attaching with them a particular political or cultural identity. As shown above, those earlier experiments did not achieve a fusion of East and West; they merely trivialized the traditions that they employed.

Further and contemporary examples are provided by some modern hotels in centres of foreign tourist interest such as Delhi and Agra. Foyers equipped with marble fountains, terraces and railings, convert the forms of Mughal architecture into a style of interior design: such schemes are no more sophisticated as a reference to tradition (even though they may be more expensive) than the interior decor of Indian restaurants in the West.

But India's more thoughtful architects are attempting to revive Indian architectural values in a more subtle manner. If they have not yet fully succeeded, this is because they are so anxious to avoid pastiche that they scarcely make any reference to the Indian tradition at all. They have generally not yet found a way of making a reference to the past which, while not being literal, still has some substance. In some cases, their references to the past are so far from being literal as to be non-existent.

An early experiment in this movement is the museum built by Charles Correa on the site of Mahatma Gandhi's *ashram* in Ahmedabad (1963) (fig. 71). For such a site, a grandiose building would have been inappropriate, and Correa's design groups a number of similar small, square huts around open courtyards. The huts are linked in a variety of ways, providing a variety of spaces, and the asymmetry of the grouping creates an informal but graceful composition. The building has been identified as one in which traditional ideas have been revived, on the ground that the simplicity of form and materials reflects Gandhian values.[25] This reflection is quite clear, but it does not constitute, of course, any reference whatever to any architectural heritage. Gandhian values are not synonymous with (or even always compatible with) those of the country's traditional architecture.

A few years later, Uttam Jain designed the University Lecture Theatres in Jodhpur (1968-72) (fig. 72). This building is a composition of considerable

71. Ahmedabad; Gandhi Ashram Museum, by Charles Correa (1963).

power; built of a local yellow sandstone, it seems to emerge from the desert sands like a strange outcrop of rock, a pyramid which encloses the students in a nether world. Jain has made full use of the intensity of the light in the region, setting dazzling planes against sharp shadows, and leaving the sun to define the crisp edges of the unmodelled and unpierced walls. The building presents a bold contrast to the architecture of Jodhpur's old city, where the light is softened and filtered through highly elaborate carving. Jain's design is therefore an original and striking conception; but it is a surprising one, perhaps, from an architect who claims (as quoted above) that his work is derivative of tradition.

However, Jain's work has attracted critics who are ready to acknowledge his success in regard to this claim. Richard Scherr, for example, argues that sensitive reference to tradition is the hallmark of Jain's projects, suggesting that such reference is discernible in the present example 'mainly through the use of the local building materials'.[26] Certainly, the stone is local, but Jodhpur's older buildings are more generally constructed of another local sandstone, which is red; and the common use of the yellow stone is recent. But this is not the only reference which Scherr detects: 'The building mass is articulated into a pattern of smaller, repetitive modules, reminiscent of certain historical prototypes typically found in Mughal palaces and mosques'. A pattern of smaller, repetitive modules can also be found in a Greek temple and in an American tower block; it is not distinctively Indian. Scherr's argument fails in the same way as some of

138

72. Jodhpur; University Lecture Theatres, by Uttam Jain (1968-72).

Curtis's claims about Le Corbusier's buildings: the inclusion of commonplace architectural motifs suggests a specific reference only to observers who are already persuaded that it must be there. Thus, as a further example, Scherr relates the stepped profile of the University Lecture Theatres to the buildings of Fatehpur Sikri and to Gujarati stepwalls; but it could be related as convincingly to Egyptian or South American prototypes. The profile here does faintly echo that of the Panch Mahal at Fatehpur Sikri, but the similarity is immediately annihilated by the blank walls, for the Panch Mahal is a pile of open pavilions.

As Scherr notes, Jain acknowledges the dominant influences on his work to have been provided by Le Corbusier and Louis Kahn.[27] Curtis's thesis that these Western Modernists were influenced by Indian architecture, retrospectively gives them a place in the Indian heritage; it blurs the distinction between Western and Indian sources, and so lends a (spurious) legitimization to their influence on younger Indian architects. But a building like Jain's lecture theatre demonstrates that that influence has tended to lead Indian architects away from, not back towards, their heritage.

The aspects of design in which contemporary Indian architects have succeeded in achieving substantial reference to tradition are planning and spatial organization. It is to these aspects that most attention has been paid: Raj Rewal explains that, in the selection of historical prototypes by architects of his generation, 'the emphasis is on the space-structure relationship';[28] and Charles Cor-

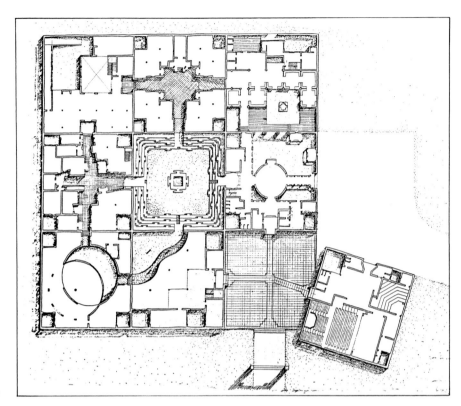

73. Jaipur; plan design
for Jawahar Kala
Kendra, by Charles
Correa (1988, revision).

rea, in an article relating his own designs to Indian antecedents, concentrates on
the definition and use of space.[29] The use of traditional planning principles is
especially pronounced in those of Correa's recent projects that he has based on a
*mandala*, a cosmological diagram proposed as a programme for the planning of
buildings by the *silpa-sastras*, the ancient Sanskrit treatises on architecture.
Among these projects is the Jawahar Kala Kendra, a cultural centre in Jaipur (designed in 1986-88) (fig. 73). The use of the nine-squared *mandala* is especially
appropriate in Jaipur, since the eighteenth-century city was itself planned on its
principles. Indeed, Correa's plan follows the local application closely: in the
building of the city, the exigencies of the site involved the dislocation of one of
the nine subdivisions, and Correa has reflected this in his own plan by detaching
one square. Correa himself identifies this reference as a successful fulfilment of
his aims: 'This is what transformation is about – producing something that is
contemporary but with roots going back'; and he intends further development
of his experiments with the theme.[30]

Western critics are eager to see the success of the movement to revive the
Indian identity, and some suggest that it is already achieved. The evidence they
present (like that of the architects themselves) refers repeatedly and almost exclusively to aspects of planning and the treatment of space. William Curtis discusses recent work by B. V. Doshi and projects by Raj Rewal in which 'spatial

organisation from past Indian architecture . . . is abstracted and transformed' (fig. 74).[31] Dan Cruickshank finds similar references in the same works, and also in works by Charles Correa and Uttam Jain.[32] The plans of new buildings are related to the clarity of a *mandala*, or the complexity of Fatehpur Sikri.

These references to tradition are real enough; they are not (like the supposed Indian features of Chandigarh) fictions created by zealous critics. Sometimes, and especially in Correa's work, the traditional planning idea has been the source of an intellectually and aesthetically satisfying design. But these references are never very substantial. The formal vocabulary of the buildings and their visual aesthetic remain Modernist and Western. The reference to traditional planning principles alone does not invest a building with an Indian identity, any more than the interpolation of an occasional *chattri* in the work of Lutyens gave that an Indian identity (though the present method is more considered). The hope that a plan can render a particular character, irrespective of the forms built on it, is somewhat optimistic. Also, in the emphasis it places on planning and the definition of space, it reflects the deep impact of the values of the Modern Movement. That emphasis is a Modernist, not an Indian, approach. Certainly, the treatment of space is a fundamental aspect of Indian, as of all, architectural design, but before the Modern Movement arrived in India, no architect (and no critic) could so entirely subordinate the treatment of form.

The character of form and detail is a subject of proper concern to the architect (and not just the obsession of the art historian) but architects in India have almost ceased discussing it. A significant reflection of this is that articles by Indian archi-

74. New Delhi; housing for the National Institute of Immunology, by Raj Rewal (1983).

tects on ancient buildings in India frequently concentrate on their planning and organization, and ignore all matters of form and decoration.[33] Such architects are interpreting their own heritage through the values of the Modernist West, assessing it by alien criteria. Some contemporary Western art historians, too, write on Indian architecture in such terms. Much recent analysis of Fatehpur Sikri, for example, presents the complex as a marvellously organized and meaningful space; no doubt it is, but it is also a marvellously wrought object, and less attention is paid to the quality of craftsmanship or the range of motifs employed.[34] There has even arisen a habit of belittling the work of the nine-teenth-century pioneer scholar Edmund Smith, who concentrated on such aspects of the complex.[35]

This approach to the Indian tradition indicates the lacuna that prevents much recent Indian architecture from containing any substantial reference to tradition. Indian architects, in their proper anxiety to avoid pastiche and through their absorption in matters of spatial organization, generally ignore entirely the detailed visual language of the Indian tradition, its forms and motifs, its habits of massing, the shapes and rhythms of its decoration. One would not wish them to insert *chajjas, chattris* or other historical forms into their buildings, for that would indeed create only pastiche; but there has been little attempt yet to transform such motifs, to adapt their practical and aesthetic functions.

For two thousand years, the compulsion to decorate buildings - with carving, paintwork or tiles – was one of the hallmarks of Indian architecture. Modern Indian architects have been reluctant to perpetuate this tradition, reluctant not only to sustain particular historical patterns and methods, but to employ any decoration at all. Perhaps it was the Modern Movement, again, which taught them to eschew it: it seems they avoid decoration because they want their build-ings to appear modern. But in regard to decoration, Modernism and the Indian tradition are fundamentally irreconcilable; clinging to the aesthetic of Moder-nism, one cannot reasonably expect to revive the Indian identity.

In 1982, Uttam Jain designed a tourist hostel for Jaisalmer (it was not built). Richard Scherr explains that Jain wished to avoid producing a facile imitation of the local buildings, and his design has elements in common with his earlier Uni-versity Lecture Theatres (fig. 72): 'The visual quality of the building is one of massive . . . planar walls with limited openings'.[36] The wish to avoid simplistic copying has sound reasons, but in Jaisalmer, of all places – historically one of the most notable centres of small-scale decorative stone carving – one cannot pro-pose massive planar walls with limited openings and claim to be following the cultural context. The inspiration of this design is perhaps hinted at in Scherr's comment that 'Jain's denial of decoration and ornament . . . would seem to firmly base his work in a mainstream, modernist camp'.[37] Similarly, William Curtis records of Raj Rewal that 'he has also been interested in Mughal palace complexes, with their repeating themes, their stratified terraces, and their fusions of primary geometries'.[38] This interest is reflected in some of Rewal's

75. New Delhi; Belgian Embassy, by Satish Gujral (1980-83).

work; but there is no indication that he has observed that what is even more distinctive of the Mughal palaces, is that they contain some of the most gorgeous architectural ornament in the world.

In addition to decoration, traditional Indian architecture typically has a sculptural quality which is quite distinct from surface ornament. There is a plasticity of forms and volumes which is especially pronounced in Hindu religious architecture. It is a feature also of the work of Le Corbusier – quite coincidentally, owing nothing to (because it pre-dates) his visits to India – but, curiously, it is the one aspect of his work not transmitted to his Indian followers. B. V. Doshi's Institute of Indology (fig. 69) lacks any such plasticity. In some of his recent work, however – including Sangath (his office in Ahmedabad; 1979-80) and the Gandhi Labour Institute in the same city (1984) – this essential Indian quality is beginning to re-surface.

It is present too in Satish Gujral's controversial design for the Belgian Embassy in Delhi (1980-83) (fig. 75). The bulging, curved forms of this building, and the appearance of great strength, echo basic elements of temple architecture. There is no literal reference to specific antecedents; as Gujral told Dan Cruickshank, 'I did not want to create anything Indian or Western; I just sat down to design'.[39] But the consequence of his impartiality is that the Indian identity has exerted itself effortlessly. That this extends to the forms of the building as well as its spatial organization unsettles some critics, who call it 'theatrical Orientalism' and 'cultural caricature'.[40] It is no such thing. It is not a pastiche as Indo-Saracenic architecture is; it is an (allegedly unconscious) evoca-

143

tion of the spirit of Indian design, comparable to Lutyens's great dome. It is one of the few recent designs that goes far enough to be successful in reviving an Indian identity; its reference to the past is at once interpretive and yet emphatic.

A third major quality, apart from decoration and plasticity, that is often missing from new Indian buildings, is good craftsmanship. One of the most striking aspects of old Indian buildings is the perfection of their detailing: a perfection not just of the decorative carving in stone and wood, but of every join and edge, flawlessly executed in fine materials which were well understood. This contrasts strongly with the poor finish of most modern buildings. The master mason capable of producing entire buildings is now an extinct species, but skilled craftsmen in lesser, decorative fields such as woodwork still survive. They are not admitted to the building site. Architects choose to have a window and its casement, say, shoddily constructed by unskilled labourers from modern materials – concrete, metal and glass – rather than use a wooden screen carved by a craftsman. The common apprehension that craft work would be an expensive alternative is simply uninformed (and curiously repeats the prejudice and ignorance of the British PWD). A visit to any handicraft emporium will reveal that skilled work can still be obtained and is remarkably inexpensive.

The movement to re-establish the identity of Indian architecture is now well established. But it will never be wholly successful unless and until it progresses resolutely beyond the imitation of traditional ways of organizing space, and re-captures some of the other seminal qualities of the Indian tradition, such as those described. It ought to be clear from the whole argument of this book that this is not a plea for the insertion of archaic motifs into buildings. As repeatedly demonstrated here, whenever such operations have been attempted in India, the results have been more or less deplorable. And although some sympathy is here shown for the aims of Revivalists such as Swinton Jacob, F. S. Growse and E. B. Havell, those aims are considered in their historical context; it would be impossible to pursue them today: a return to the guild system could not now be effected even if it were desired.

The present argument is just that if the retrieval of the Indian identity is to succeed fully, the country's architects must escape more thoroughly than they have yet done from the values of the Modern Movement, and must recover those enduring values of their own tradition that the Modern Movement taught them to abhor. Decoration might be revived, not through the reproduction of antique temple sculpture or Islamic tiles, but through the evolution of a new repertoire from a range of historical sources (and perhaps also from vernacular traditions, which survive); the sterile utilitarian aspect of Modernism might give way to a more plastic aesthetic; and the craftsman might be permitted to contribute his knowledge and skill with materials. The idea that such traditional values are not applicable to large modern buildings, is no more true now than it has been at any time in the last one hundred years.

That such a recovery is feasible is suggested by a comparison with other cultural regions. In parts of the Islamic world (especially the geographically more westerly parts, including Egypt and Saudi Arabia), architects are returning to traditional patterns, not only of planning, but of form and decoration, and sometimes even technology; and yet they are developing a distinctly modern Islamic style. A similar process can be observed in Japan. In India, the task is more difficult. The cultural identity is buried deeper, because it has been suppressed not only by Modernism but by a long period of culturally antagonistic colonial rule. But it was an identity of formidable power, and there are a few signs that it is not altogether lost, that it may yet return to its former vigour.

## The Cultural Memory

The recent buildings discussed above house institutions, not private individuals; they correspond in function to the public buildings of the nineteenth century, and, like them, they chiefly reflect the concerns of a few sophisticated architects. To find reflections of the attitudes of the bulk of the educated classes, we must seek examples of new domestic architecture, the counterparts of the Shekhavati *haveli* or PWD-style bungalow. Charles Correa and Raj Rewal have been commissioned to design housing schemes in Bombay and Delhi, in which they continue their revivalist experiments. But in the fashionable residential enclaves of these cities, the commonest type of house is still what it has been for the last thirty years. This type is functional and modern; its elements are entirely orthogonal, but the right angles wander in a way dictated by function, with no regard to composition or even coherence. In one sense, such a house is a remarkable achievement, for it appears to have been designed with no regard to style whatever.

In recent years, some dissatisfaction with this state of affairs has developed. Some householders are tired of all houses appearing much the same, and wish to invest their own with some individuality, some style even. Here, too, there is a quest for identity, but there is also an uncertainty about where it is to come from. A result of these feelings is the growth of a style of house known in Delhi as Punjabi Baroque.[41] This style grafts onto a Modernist frame details gathered from a welter of sources: typically, Spanish arcades jostle with Swiss chalet eaves and classical porticoes (fig. 76). Whatever source Punjabi Baroque plunders, it abuses, turning its forms into meretricious ornaments. The only source that it does not often use is the Indian tradition; it does not, for example, imitate the plan or forms of the *haveli*, although those traditional elements are better suited to the urban environment than the detached bungalow. This obvious potential source is ignored, because (as Malay Chatterjee's remark about indigenization suggests) there is a qualm that the use of native sources might appear backward.

In his attitude to his own cultural heritage, the educated Indian has been consistently held in a cleft stick by Western influence. As recounted above, during

76. New Delhi; a
modern private house in
a residential suburb.

the period of colonial rule, while the colonial power was Westernizing India's
educated classes, Britons not only derided the Indian heritage, they also mocked
the Westernized Indian for the inaccuracy of his imitation of Western tastes.
Even Macaulay, who turned the process of Westernization into a deliberate
policy, was scornful of the effects of the process that were already visible when
he arrived in the country:

> I was honoured by an interview with the Rajah of Mysore, who insisted
> on showing me all his wardrobe, and his picture gallery. He has six or
> seven coloured English prints not much inferior to those which I have seen
> in the sanded parlour of a country inn; 'Going to Cover', 'The Death of
> the Fox', and so forth. But the bijou of his gallery, of which he is as vain
> as the Grand Duke can be of the Venus, . . . is a head of the Duke of
> Wellington, which has, most certainly, been on a sign-post in England.[42]

If there was no right choice for the educated Indian in the colonial period, the
situation is scarcely better now. Since Independence, the West, having previously persuaded him to discard his own heritage as worthless, now informs
him that it was not worthless after all, but precious; and it encourages him to
rescue it from the refuse pile rather than pursue poor imitations of the West. But
at the same time, the West, still politically and economically the dominant sector
of the world, continues passively to present a cultural model. In these circumstances, an educated Indian might be forgiven for being unsure whether he will
find a greater self-respect in continuing to follow Western tastes or in returning
to his heritage.

In recent times, the Indian heritage has generally commanded more respect among Westerners than among educated Indians. Western tourists provide patronage to surviving handicraft traditions, as the proliferation of tourist shops full of such work shows. Often this craft work is of a very high quality, and it is growing in quantity too. Many urban Indians find it difficult to admire this work; but there is a growing number who do, who are beginning to re-examine their heritage, to redecorate their homes with Indian furnishings and objects, to return to traditional styles of clothing, to grow interested in architectural conservation. It is ironic that there is an element of Western influence in this change: the West, having once wanted the East to be like itself, now wants it to be different, and encourages this indigenization through its conspicuous respect for Indian cultural patterns. But the change springs also, and more fundamentally, from the growing awareness among Indians that imitation of the West can never be wholly successful or satisfying, and that in the attempt much of genuine value and unique character is lost.

In 1961, Edward Shils remarked that, often in Asian societies, 'the intellectual elites adhere to elements of cultural patterns which, whether they are potentially harmonious with the autochthonous traditional cultural pattern or not, are not at present actually harmonious with those traditions'.[43] A change which has been taking place in parts of Asia since then is that the intellectual elites have begun to care more about the potential for such harmony. A nineteenth-century maharaja or nawab was not much bothered about whether the Westernized tastes he developed were in harmony with traditional cultural patterns, because so far as he developed such tastes, he happily abandoned those patterns. Options do not have to be in harmony. But to an increasing number of educated Indians, the possibility of harmony is a matter of great importance, because they do not wish to have to choose. They wish to retain both the modernity that is the gift of the West, and the distinct cultural identity that is the legacy from their ancestors. These things must be resolved if Indians are to lead undivided lives.

Until a few years ago, it seemed that the old cliché that India's ancient civilization could absorb any foreign influence and make it part of itself, had finally been exposed as a fallacy. The influence of the West had seemingly cracked the civilization and the society apart, severing the educated elite both from their cultural roots and from the mass of the population who adhered to those roots at a peasant level.[44] But at present, there are signs that the cliché will be reinstated, that Indian civilization will yet come to terms with Western influence, as the wound heals and the cultural memory is gradually recovered.

# Notes

## Chapter One: 'An Unsuccessful Attempt at the Grecian'

1. Quoted in Archer 1980, p. 139. Archer argued that the aquatint, published in London in 1797, was based on drawings made on the spot between 1786 and 1788.
2. A drawing of this building was presented to the RIBA by the Raja's son in 1838. It is reproduced in Archer 1963, p. 321; Archer 1968, p. 63; and Nilsson 1968, pl. 76.
3. Fergusson 1862, p. 418.
4. This *pietra dura* work is discussed, and an iconological interpretation of it proposed, by Koch 1988.
5. Nilsson 1968, p. 100.
6. For example, by Fergusson 1862, p. 419; Nilsson 1968, p. 131; Davies 1985, p. 93; Llewellyn-Jones 1985, pp. 140, 158.
7. For example, by Nilsson 1968, p. 131; and Davies 1985, p. 91. For earlier instances of this idea, see Llewellyn-Jones 1985, pp. 140-42.
8. This obsession is discussed by Llewellyn-Jones 1985, pp. 139-40.
9. Fergusson 1862, p. 419; and Nilsson 1968, p. 131.
10. The influence of Constantia has been recognized by many writers, including Fergusson 1910, vol. 2, p. 326; Sharar 1975, p. 52; Tandan 1978, p. 348; and Llewellyn-Jones 1985, p. 135. The Residency, by contrast, has been generally overlooked as a possible influence on Nawabi architecture. This is perhaps explained by its ruined state: the Residency was the scene of one of the most famous episodes of the mutiny of 1857, in the course of which it was substantially destroyed, and the ruin has stood as a memorial ever since. Its condition makes assessment of its influence difficult. Llewellyn-Jones (1985, p. 114) made this point, but went on to dismiss its possible influence on the ground that the Residency buildings were 'eclectic' in style (though she adduced no evidence for that assertion). It seems reasonable to suppose that a building with the prestige of the Resident attached to it would have been noticed as much as Constantia (even it it was intrinsically less impressive), especially since the Nawabs had to pay for it.
11. The identity of the designer of the Residency is not known, but Nilsson conjectured reasonably (1968, p. 113) that an English engineer directed Indian masons.
12. This tomb is more generally known as the Shah Najaf Imambara.
13. See Llewellyn-Jones 1985, pp. 144, 145, and pl. 18.
14. For example, by Tandan 1978, pp. 150, 355; and Meade 1987, p. 28.
15. Fergusson 1862, p. 420; repeated in idem, 1910, vol. 2, p. 327.
16. Fergusson 1910, vol. 2, p. 324.
17. Fergusson 1862, p. 420; repeated in idem 1910, vol. 2, p. 326.
18. Sharar 1975, pp. 51-52.
19. H.G. Keene in 1875, quoted in Tandan 1978, p. 315.
20. John Terry in 1958, quoted in ibid., p. 318.
21. Ibid., pp. 169, 355.
22. Llewellyn-Jones 1985, p. 235.
23. Ibid., p. 227.
24. Ibid., p. 235.
25. See, for example, Fergusson's comparison of the Parthenon with the temple of Halebid (Fergusson 1910, vol. 1, pp. 448-50). From this comparison, he concluded that 'the great value of the study of these Indian examples is that it widens so immensely our basis for architectural criticism. It is only by becoming familiar with forms so utterly dissimilar from those we have hitherto been conversant with, that we perceive how narrow is the

purview that is content with one form or one passing fashion'.

26. Llewellyn-Jones 1985, p. 146.
27. Tandan 1978, pp. 354-55.
28. Llewellyn-Jones 1985, pp. vi, 192, 239.
29. To give (with no invidious intent) one example, this view of architectural expression is found as an unquestioned assumption in the writing on architecture of James Morris, writing otherwise characterized by urbanity and sensitivity. Consider the observation that '. . . the Empire was taking a Gothic turn. Its style, in life as in art, was becoming more elaborate, more assertive. . .'. (James Morris, *Heaven's Command* (1973), repr.: Harmondsworth 1979, pp. 266-67).
30. In the process of (quite properly) castigating those who suppose that 'architectural decadence' is the unavoidable expression of a political or moral decadence, Llewellyn-Jones (1985, p. 192) doubted whether such a thing as architectural decadence exists. If by this she meant that the word 'decadence', with its moral overtones, is poorly chosen, because it encourages an identification between morals and aesthetics, then her doubt is a fair one. But many people who describe an architecture as 'decadent' really mean that it is debased, not in a moral sense, but more as coinage can be debased. Debased architecture might be defined as architecture evidently derived from a once powerful tradition but lacking in design the power of its antecedents. If we deny that debased architecture exists – if, in an effort at broadmindedness, we deny that some buildings are inferior to others – then we deny ourselves the right to make aesthetic judgments at all, we adopt a relativism which accepts the bad along with the good. In short, if there is no such thing as debased architecture, there is no such thing as taste.
31. This line of defence, though expressed nowhere in print to the author's knowledge, has been expressed to him personally; and it exemplifies a popular approach to architectural history in general.
32. Such as Llewellyn-Jones 1985, p. 236.
33. Sharar 1975, p. 52.
34. See, for example, Llewellyn-Jones 1985, pp. 236-37. A similar comparison between the Royal Pavilion and Indian hybrid experiments was made by Nilsson (1968, p. 164).
35. A more apt comparison might be drawn between the Lucknow mixed style and Tudor attempts at classicism. The latter are likewise often interesting historical curiosities but seldom good architecture.

(Such a comparison was made, without disparagement, by Havell 1913, p. 238.)
36. Fergusson 1910, vol. 2, p. 185.
37. Sharma 1980, p. 33.
38. The term 'Marwari' originally meant 'of Marwar' (i.e. Jodhpur) and was applied to merchants who came from that state; it has long been used more widely to refer to merchants from northern Rajasthan in general.
39. Nath and Wacziarg (1982, p. 106) pointed out that, though the first railways in India were laid in in the 1850s, they did not reach Shekhavati until 1916; many of the depictions of trains on the *havelis* predate this, and must therefore have been based on descriptions rather than observation – a fact which may account for their often fanciful nature.
40. Recorded by Sanderson 1913, p. 15.

## Chapter Two: Pax Britannica and the New Breed

1. See, for example, the original treaty between the East India Company and the Maharana of Udaipur, published in Tod 1972, vol 1, appendix, p. 631. The treaty with the Maharaja of Bikaner is published in Sehgal 1972, pp. 69-71.
2. See Tod 1972, vol. 1, appendix, p. 631; Sehgal 1972, pp. 69-70.
3. These statistics were given by the Maharaja of Baroda (Baroda 1980, p. 111).
4. Quoted in Trevelyan 1876, vol. 1, p. 403.
5. See ibid., vol. 1, p. 423.
6. Ibid., vol. 1, p. 323.
7. Ibid., vol. 1, pp. 428-49.
8. Quoted ibid., vol. 1, pp. 443-44.
9. Ibid., vol. 1, p. 381.
10. Laurie 1888, p. 173.
11. Macaulay did not say which works he had read. Those then available in translation included the *Ramayana*, translated by Joshua Marshman and W. Carey in 1806-10, and the *Bhagavad Gita*, translated by C. Wilkins in 1785. Among the works of Kalidas, *Sakuntala* was available in a translation by William Jones (1789) and *Meghaduta* in a translation by H.H. Wilson (1813). The great Persian history of India by Ferishta had been translated by Alexander Dow (published 1786-72).
12. Quoted in Trevelyan, 1876, vol. 1, p. 372.
13. Quoted ibid., vol. 1, pp. 445-46.
14. Laurie 1888, p. 181.
15. The minute is quoted in full ibid., pp. 170-84.
16. Quoted ibid., p. 175.
17. Quoted ibid., p. 175.
18. See, for example, Rahman 1973. Rahman argued

(pp. 53, 66) that, in the late medieval period, in-dividual scientific inquiry in India was on a par with that in Europe, but that India lacked the in-stitutional base – the academies and societies – that in Europe enabled scientific discovery to become cumulative.

19. Laurie 1888, p. 183.
20. Sleeman 1844, vol. 2, pp. 36–37. The same episode is recorded by Fergusson 1910, vol. 2, p. 308, n.1.
21. Fergusson 1910, vol. 2, p. 287; see also p. 298.
22. Ruskin 1903-12, vol. 16, p. 262.
23. Ibid., pp. 265-66.
24. The objection to Indian art on the ground of its per-ceived antipathy to Nature was, of course, con-sistent with Ruskin's general theories of art. (The perception, incidentally, was not based on a wide acquaintance with Indian art and is belied by much – by the sculpture of Sanchi, for example.) In the second lecture of *The Two Paths*, Ruskin pro-claimed that Indian art aims not at Nature but only at pleasure, and that 'the art whose end is pleasure only is pre-eminently the gift of cruel and savage nations' (ibid., p. 306). The embryo of these ideas can be found in a work from Ruskin's youth, namely *Salsette and Elephanta*, his Newdigate Prize poem of 1839. This prematurely celebrates the con-version of India to Christianity and describes the sculptures of Elephanta as 'forms of fear . . . wreathed groups of dim, distorted life'. See *The Works of John Ruskin*, ed. by E.T. Cook and Alex-ander Wedderburn, London, 1903-12, vol. 2, p. 94. See also ibid., vol. 16, pp. 304-307; vol. 20, pp, 227, 231, 349.
25. See Gupta 1981, p. 26.
26. Quoted ibid., p. 57. The development is also described by Fergusson, 1910, vol. 2, p. 312.
27. Conner 1979, p. 171.
28. See Head 1985.
29. Birdwood 1880, p. 125; *Imperial Gazetteer* 1908-1909, vol. 2, p. 121.
30. Coomaraswamy 1985, p. 68.
31. See *The Works of John Ruskin* (note 24), vol. 20, p. 231.
32. Hodges 1794, p. 64. Hodges first published these views in his *Dissertation on the Prototypes of Architec-ture, Hindoo, Moorish, and Gothic* of 1787.
33. Bernier 1914, p. 299.
34. Sleeman 1844, vol. 2, p. 32.
35. Even Sleeman (ibid., vol. 2, p. 34) believed the theory that the Taj Mahal was designed by Austin of Bordeaux. See also Vincent Smith, *A History of Fine Art in India and Ceylon*, 2d ed. (Oxford, 1930), pp. 183-85; and Tillotson 1986.
36. See Conner 1979, p. 114.
37. Maffey 1903, p. 3. John Lockwood Kipling had earlier made the same observation: see J.L. Kipling 1886, p. 1.
38. Quoted in Nilsson 1968, p. 105.
39. These plans are discussed ibid., pp. 110-11.
40. J.L. Kipling 1886, p. 3.
41. Havell 1913, p. 226.
42. See Sir Lepel Griffin, *Famous Monuments of Central India* (London, 1886), p. 68.
43. Davies 1985, p. 107.
44. These buildings are discussed ibid., pp. 155-64.
45. Fergusson 1910, vol. 2, p. 332.
46. Burgess 1876, p. 176.
47. According to an inscription on the Wazir's own tomb.
48. See Stamp 1981, p. 358; Metcalf 1984; and Davies 1985, pp. 192-93.
49. The present writer has elsewhere (Tillotson 1987a, p. 203) argued for its abandonment, but on further reflection urges its retention: its very stupidity gives it a certain aptness.
50. The circumstances of the design and construction of Mayo College are fully described by Metcalf 1984, pp. 45-56.
51. It has even been argued (ibid., p. 50) that, by employing an Indian style in this context, the British, far from granting a concession, were pro-claiming themselves masters of Indian civilization.
52. Quoted in Baroda 1980, p. 156.
53. Chisholm 1883, p. 141.
54. Quoted in Metcalf, 1984, p. 49.
55. See, for example, Meade 1987, pp. 29-30; and Davies 1985, pp. 192-204.
56. See Davies 1985, p. 243; and Head 1986, p. 38.
57. See Mant's remarks quoted in Metcalf 1984, p. 49.
58. Chisholm 1883, p. 141.
59. For accounts of Griffin's work in India, see James Birell, *Walter Burley Griffin* (Queensland, 1964), pp. 177-81; and Donald Leslie Johnson, *The Archi-tecture of Walter Burley Griffin* (South Melbourne, 1977), pp. 126-37. The author is grateful to Susan Rossen for drawing Griffin's work to his attention.
60. Quoted in Birrell, op. cit. p. 178.
61. Quoted in Baroda 1980, p. 48.
62. Ibid.

## Chapter Three: The Indian Revival

1. Quoted in Davies 1985, p. 197.
2. By the architect René Phene Spiers, cited in Head 1986, p. 75.

3. See ibid., p. 79.
4. Chisholm 1883, p. 141. See also Stamp 1981, p. 367; Davies, 1985, p. 197; Head 1986, p. 75; Kagal 1986, p. 103.
5. Havell 1913, pp. 230-31.
6. See, for example, Brown 1942, vol. 2, p. 125; Stamp 1981, pp. 368-69. See also the references to Jacob's work in Metcalf 1984, p. 58; and Head 1986, p. 76 (though both these authors have given just accounts of Growse's work). See also below, notes 31 and 68.
7. For an account of the military Jacobs, see Callahan 1978.
8. R. Kipling 1907, vol. 1, p. 34.
9. See Sen 1878, p. 1; Showers 1916, p. 32.
10. For accounts of Jaipur blue pottery, see A. Nath 1986; and A. Nath and Wacziarg 1987, pp. 186-205.
11. See Sen 1878, pp. 2-5; Showers 1916, pp. 33-34.
12. The exhibition was held in the building on Sireh Deori Bazaar, now known as the Sawai Man Singh II Town Hall: see Hendley, 1884, vol. 3, captions to pls. 190, 191, 195. Some writers have wrongly assumed that the exhibition was held in the Albert Hall (now the City Museum).
13. Ibid., vol. 1, p.v. Hendley's intention has been misunderstood; it has even been assumed that he was showing Indian craftsmen objects of European manufacture, and so contributed to the debasement of the Indian arts (A. Nath and Wacziarg 1982, p. 31).
14. See Hendley 1896a, p. 1; Jain and Jain 1935, chap. 17, p. 7; and Sarkar 1984, p. 367.
15. Hendley 1896a, p. 1.
16. Hendley in Showers 1916, pp. 29-30; (for the attribution of this passage to Hendley, see Showers's preface).
17. Ibid., p. 32.
18. Ibid., p. 26.
19. R. Kipling 1907, vol. 1, pp. 39-43.
20. Ibid., vol. 1, p. 40.
21. *Jeypore State Public Works Reports* 1876, pp. 2-3; 1877, p. 3; 1878, pp. 4-5.
22. Ibid., 1879, p. 7
23. Ibid., 1881, p. 9.
24. Ibid., 1883, p. 16; 1884, p. 15; Showers 1916, p. 80.
25. Hendley 1896a, p. 1; Jain and Jain 1935, chap. 17, p. 8.
26. Hendley 1896a, p. 2.
27. Jacob in Showers 1916, p. 80; (for the attribution of this passage to Jacob, see Showers's preface).
28. Hendley 1884, vol. 1, p. 55.

29. Jacob 1890-1913, pt. 11, index and pls. 12, 46-56.
30. R. Kipling 1907, vol. 1, p. 37.
31. Metcalf 1984, p. 50. See also Jain and Jain 1935, chap. 17, p. 6; and note 6 above. It is true that Hendley (1896a, p. 1) described the building as Indo-Saracenic, but he of course used that term in a broader sense, as Fergusson used it – i.e. 'in the style of late medieval India' – and so he did not thereby particularly associate the Albert Hall with the work of Chisholm and Mant et al. To the modern writer, the term has (or ought to have) this more specific reference. See also the discussion in Chapter Two, p. 46.
32. Davies 1985, p. 15.
33. *Jeypore State Public Works Reports* 1884, p. 15.
34. See Sen 1878, p. 6; Jacob 1890-1913, pt. 11, preface.
35. Jacob referred to this arrangement in a letter of 27 March 1896, addressed to the Secretary of the Council (see Jaipur ... Records, in Rajasthan State Archives, ser. no. 256). See also supplements to *Jeypore State Public Works Reports*, 1888. The retirement, after twenty-six years, in 1899, of both Ghasi Ram and Mir Tujumool Hoosein is recorded ibid., 1899, p. 15.
36. Ibid., 1883, pp. 16, 3.
37. Jacob 1890-1913, pt. 1, preface.
38. Ibid., pt. 1, preface.
39. Cited in Tarapor 1982, p. 45.
40. Fergusson 1862, p. 413.
41. Byron 1931a, pp. 14, 1.
42. R. Kipling 1907, vol. 1, p. 10.
43. Notably Stamp 1976, 1981; Davies 1985; and Morris 1986.
44. Jacob 1890-1913, pt. 1, preface
45. Sehgal 1972, pp. 59-63.
46. Chisholm 1883, p. 141.
47. Sanderson 1913, p. 16.
48. Elsewhere (Tillotson 1987a, p. 203), the present writer has referred to the Jodhpur Court without acknowledging the involvement of Jacob, and citing it as an example of Indo-Saracenic work; it should not be so designated, because of the involvement of Indian craftsmen in its design (see Sanderson 1913, p. 19).
49. As stated in note 12 above, the building is now known as the Sawai Man Singh II Town Hall. Its design was attributed to Jacob by Hendley 1884, vol. 1, p. viii.
50. Hendley 1896a, p. 4. For some of Birdwood's views on Indian fine art, see chp. 2, note 29, above.
51. *Jeypore State Public Works Reports*, 1902, p. 24. The

date of Jacob's final departure from Jaipur is not known.

52. Sanderson 1913, p. 17. For details of the Raj Imarat and Chiman Lal, see *Jeypore State Public Works Reports*, 1890, p. 3; 1901, p. 4. It will be noticed that no contemporary source attributes the design of the Mubarak Mahal to Jacob. Chaubey Biswesarnath, ex-Secretary to the Jaipur State Council, writing in Jain and Jain 1935, chap. 17, acknowledged Jacob's role in the design of the Albert hall (p. 6), but made no mention of him when discussing the Mubarak Mahal (pp. 2-3).

53. Sanderson 1913, p. 18.

54. For a discussion of *mandala* planning in Rajput architecture, see Tillotson 1987a, pp. 79-85, 169-74.

55. There is a local tradition that the Rajendra Pol was built during the reign of Maharaja Sawai Ram Singh (1835-80); and elsewhere (ibid. p. 215, n. 49), the present writer has followed that tradition. But this is probably wrong: the gate is related in both function and style to the Mubarak Mahal, with which it is therefore, most likely, contemporary.

56. See *Jeypore State Public Works Reports,* 1912, p. 21.

57. Growse 1880, p. vi and n.

58. Ibid., p. 149n.

59. Ibid., p. 150.

60. Ibid., pp. 510-11.

61. Ibid., pp. ii, iii, 151.

62. Ibid., pp. 162, 154, 511.

63. Growse 1886, caption to pl. 28.

64. Ibid., caption to pl. 32.

65. Ibid., caption to pl. 32. This attitude towards Western influence represents something of a shift from Growse's earlier view that a synthesis of Indian and Western ideas was positively desirable, and might give India a new architecture akin to that developed under Akbar's patronage through a synthesis of Hindu and Islamic ideas (see Growse 1880, pp. 160-61).

66. Clarke 1884, p. 782.

67. Growse 1886, caption to pl. 23.

68. Davies 1985, p. 194; see also note 6 above. The association of Growse with the Indo-Saracenic movement has been previously criticized by Tarapor 1982, p. 51.

69. Growse 1886, p. 6.

70. The original pamphlet was entitled *Bulandshahr or Sketches of an Indian District* (Nov. 1884); the revised work was published in two volumes in 1885-86.

71. Growse 1886, p. ii.

72. Ibid., p. iii.

73. Ibid.

74. Ibid., p. ii. The gate in question might be the building later illustrated by John Lockwood Kipling (see fig. 18).

75. Ibid., appendix, pp. 7-8. The list of subscribers to the cost of the Mathura church is given in Growse 1880, pp. 508-509; Growse contributed over one-third of the total.

76. Growse 1886, p. ii, appendix, pp, 9-10.

77. Ibid., appendix, p. 10.

78. Ibid., appendix, pp. 5-6, 11.

79. Ibid., p. ii.

80. Ibid., appendix, p. 6.

81. Ibid., p. i.

82. Birdwood 1880, p. 132; see also pp. 133-37.

83. The Resolution of 14 March 1883 was published in *The Journal of Indian Art* 1, 1 (1886), preface.

84. Growse 1886, pp. i-ii, iii.

85. For example, by Stamp, 1981, p. 363; and Davies 1985, p. 163.

86. For a fuller account of de Forest's operations, see Head, 1986, pp. 101-109; and Head 1988, pp. 123-26.

87. De Forest 1885, introduction.

88. Watt 1903, p. 1.

89. Fergusson 1862, p. 408.

90. Clarke 1884, p. 782.

91. Quoted in Growse 1886, press notices, p. 5.

92. J.L. Kipling 1886, p. 1.

93. Ibid., p. 2.

94. Ibid., p. 4.

95. Maffey 1903, p. 4.

96. Ibid., pp. 32-34.

97. See also, for example, Watt 1903, p. 65.

98. See, for example, Havell 1913, pp. 235, 242. Havell gave an account of Growse's work, pp. 233-35.

99. Ibid., p. 222.

100. Ibid., pp. 222-23, 244.

101. Callahan 1978, pp. 10-11.

## Chapter Four: The Crossroads on Raisina

1. Quoted in Irving 1981, p. 11.

2. *The Parliamentary Debates,* 5th ser. vol. 11, pp. 162-63.

3. Lady Hardinge, quoted in M. Lutyens 1980, p. 113.

4. *The Parliamentary Debates,* 5th ser. vol. 41, pp. 1910, 1919.

5. M. Lutyens 1980, p. 115.

6. Begg 1913, p. 5.

7. Byron 1931a, p. 14.
8. *The Builder,* 27 Sep. 1912, p. 345.
9. *The Times,* 3 Oct. 1912, p. 7.
10. Baker 1912, p. 8.
11. Irving 1981, p. 42
12. M. Lutyens 1980, p. 104.
13. Quoted in Irving 1981, p. 98.
14. M. Lutyens 1980, pp. 108, 111, 116, 118-9.
15. *The Parliamentary Debates,* 5th ser. vol. 44, pp. 277, 813-14, 2103-2110; vol. 45, pp. 228-29, 1271, 1945-50, 1952-53.
16. Havell 1913, p. vi.
17. Ibid., 248-9.
18. Ibid., p. 252.
19. Havell 1927, pp. 274-75.
20. Sanderson 1913, p. 6.
21. Ibid., pp. 11-12, 9.
22. Begg 1913, p. 5.
23. Ibid., pp. 1, 2-3, 4-5.
24. Stamp 1981, p. 371. Havell 1927, pp. 260-61, later recorded how Begg was converted to an admiration for Indian craftsmen when he inadvertently left some to their own devices.
25. *The Parliamentary Debates,* 5th ser. vol. 46, p. 976; vol 47, pp. 190, 1658-60, 1800, 1963-64; vol. 51, p. 187; vol. 54, p. 185; vol. 55, pp. 197-98, 1040; vol. 56, pp. 516-17.
26. Published in Havell 1927, p. 275.
27. Begg 1913, Preface.
28. Lanchester 1923, p. 293.
29. Ibid., p. 294.
30. Ibid., pp. 304, 306-308. Looking back a few years later, A.G. Shoosmith also asserted that the Indian master builder had long been extinct, a situation for which he blamed the Mughal Emperor Aurangzeb. See Shoosmith 1938, p. 208.
31. Havell 1913, pp. 252-53; Begg 1913, p. 5.
32. Lanchester 1923, p. 304.
33. M. Lutyens 1980, p. 143.
34. Quoted in Irving 1981, p. 107.
35. Stamp 1981, p. 377.
36. Havell 1927, p. 264
37. Cited ibid., p. 263.
38. Shoosmith 1938, p. 208; Brown 1942, vol. 2, p. 126.
39. Irving 1981, p. 87.
40. Quoted ibid., p. 280.
41. M. Lutyens 1980, p. 114.
42. Baker 1912, p. 7.
43. Metcalf's argument (1984, p. 61) that the fundamentally classical character of the New Delhi buildings marked the end of Indo-Saracenic architecture, ignores the fact that, to some of its ex-ponents, the essence of the Indo-Saracenic experiment was to graft Indian details onto a Western structure.
44. Byron 1931a, p. 18. See also Davies 1985, p. 232.
45. Byron 1931a, p. 30; Shoosmith 1938, p. 208; and Stamp 1976. p. 370. See also Bence-Jones 1973, p. 197; Irving 1981, p. 170; and Davies 1985; p. 226.
46. For example, by Irving 1981, p. 142; Moorhouse 1983, pp. 236-37; Davies 1985, p. 231; and Morris 1986, p. 220.
47. The work of Medd and Shoosmith in Delhi is discussed and illustrated by Stamp 1976; and Irving 1981, pp. 319-38.
48. Quoted in Christopher Hussey, *The Life of Sir Edwin Lutyens* (London, 1950), p. 247.
49. Quoted in Stamp 1981, p. 373.
50. Ibid., p. 373.
51. There are, or course, other issues which might be discussed in relation to the buildings of New Delhi, such as their relevance to the needs and aspirations of the people of India at the beginning of the century, and whether the visible approach of Independence as they were built ought to have brought modifications to the scheme; but such questions lie outside the scope of the present discussion of style and method.

## *Chapter Five: Independence and Dependence*

1. Shoosmith 1938, p. 209. Shoosmith, while lamenting the extinction of Indian architectural identity, did not see Lutyens's idiom as a part of the 'heaped chaos of foreign importations' that had brought it about. The works he had in mind may have included those of Walter Burley Griffin; see p. 57.
2. See, for example, the comments of B.V. Doshi in Kagal 1986, p. 211; and those of Prasad 1987, pp. 281-82.
3. See, for example, Charles Correa's remarks quoted in Ahuja 1987, p. 19; and Prasad 1987, p. 282.
4. Ibid., p. 286.
5. William Curtis, 'The Ancient in the Modern', in Rewal 1985, p. 81.
6. Ibid., pp. 84-89.
7. See Correa quoted in Ahuja 1987, p. 18; Prasad 1987 pp. 283-4, 286, 295; Pethe 1987, p. 17.
8. Quoted in Prasad 1987, pp. 283, 280.
9. See ibid., pp. 283-84, 293, 297.
10. For example, by Ram Sharma in Rewal 1985, p. 112; Correa in Ahuja 1987, p. 15; Pethe 1987, p. 17; and Uttam Jain in Scherr 1987, p. 10.
11. Doshi in Kagal 1986, p. 212.

12. Curtis 1987, pp. 34, 35.
13. Batley 1973, p. 7.
14. Radio broadcast by Batley, quoted in Rewal 1985, p. 54.
15. Dhama 1956, introduction (unpag.).
16. Cf. Stamp 1981, p. 367.
17. Brown 1942, vol. 2, p. 127.
18. Quoted in Ahuja 1987, p. 15.
19. Rewal in Rewal 1985, p. 12.
20. Both ibid., pp. 12-23, 112-23. See also Pethe 1987.
21. Correa 1987, p. 174.
22. Quoted in Scherr 1987, p. 12.
23. Malay Chatterjee in Rewal 1985, p. 124.
24. See the comments (perhaps by Correa) on New Delhi in Kagal 1986, p. 106.
25. Ibid., p. 168.
26. Scherr 1987.
27. Ibid., p. 10.
28. Rewal 1985, p. 12.
29. Correa 1987, pp. 166-70
30. Quoted in Cruickshank 1987, p. 57; and letter to the author, Oct. 1988.
31. Curtis 1987, pp. 36, 38.
32. Cruickshank 1987, pp. 54-58.
33. See, for example, various articles in Rewal 1985, pp. 41-57.
34. See, for example, papers in Michael Brand and Glenn D. Lowry, *Fatehpur Sikri,* Bombay, 1987.
35. See ibid., p. 122; Rewal 1985, p. 22.
36. Scherr 1987, p. 19.
37. Ibid., p. 14.
38. Curtis 1987, p. 36.
39. Cruickshank 1987, p. 52.
40. See Curtis 1987, p. 37.
41. The coining of this term is attributed to the architectural writer Gautam Bhatia; it refers to the preponderance of Punjabis among Delhi's commercial elite.
42. Quoted in Trevelyan 1876, vol. 1, p. 369.
43. Shils 1961, p. 10.
44. These issues are discussed in Naipaul 1977.

## Illustration Acknowledgements

The following plates are reproduced by kind permission of the authorities named:

1, 3, 16, 26, 50, 53, 56: The British Library; 17: Raymond Head; 18, 29, 51, 52, 54: the Syndics of Cambridge University Library; 31: Yaduendra Sahai; 33, 34, 42: Maharaja Sawai Man Singh II Museum, Jaipur; 44: Sarah Tillotson; 57: Country Life; 73: Charles Correa; 74: Dan Cruickshank. All other plates are by the author.

# Bibliography

| | |
|---|---|
| Agarawala 1979. | R. A. Agarawala. *History, Art and Architecture of Jaisalmer.* Delhi, 1979. |
| Agarwal 1979. | B. D. Agarwal. *Jodhpur* (Rajasthan District Gazetteers). Jaipur, 1979. |
| Ahuja 1987. | Sarayu Ahuja. 'Le Corbusier's Legacy: An Interview with Charles Correa'. *Indian Architect and Builder* 1, 3 (Oct. 1987), pp. 14-19. |
| Allen Dwivedi 1984. | Charles Allen and Sharada Dwivedi. *Lives of the Indian Princes.* London, 1984. |
| Archer 1963. | Mildred Archer. '"Company" Architects and Their Influence in India'. *The Journal of the Royal Institute of British Architects* 70, 8 (Aug. 1963), pp. 317-21. |
| Archer 1968. | Idem. *Indian Architecture and the British.* Middlesex, 1968. |
| Archer 1980. | Idem. *Early Views of India: The Picturesque Journeys of Thomas and William Daniell 1786-1794.* London, 1980. |
| Baker 1912. | Herbert Baker. 'The New Delhi – Eastern and Western Architecture – A Problem of Style'. *The Times,* 3 Oct. 1912, pp. 7-8. |
| Baroda 1980. | Maharaja of Baroda. *The Palaces of India.* London, 1980. |
| Batley 1973. | Claude Batley. *The Design Development of Indian Architecture.* 3d ed.: London, 1973. Originally pub. London, 1934. |
| Begg 1913. | See Sanderson 1913. |
| Bence-Jones 1973. | Mark Bence-Jones. *Palaces of the Raj.* London, 1973. |
| Bernier 1914. | François Bernier. *Travels in the Mogul Empire AD 1656-1668.* 2d ed.: rev. by Vincent Smith, Oxford, 1914. Originally pub. Paris 1670. 1st Eng. ed.: trans. by Archibald Constable, London, 1891. |
| Birdwood 1880. | George C. M. Birdwood. *The Industrial Arts of India.* London, 1880. |
| Brown 1942 | Percy Brown, *Indian Architecture.* 2 vols. Bombay, 1942. |
| Burgess 1876. | James Burgess. *Report on the Antiquities of Kathiawad and Kachh.* Archaeological Survey of Western India. Vol. 2. London, 1876. |
| Byron 1931a. | Robert Byron. 'New Delhi'. *The Architectural Review* 49 (Jan. 1931), pp. 1-30. |
| Byron 1931b. | Idem. 'New Delhi'. *Country Life* 69 (1931), pp. 708-16, 754-61, 782-89, 808-15. |
| Callahan 1978. | Raymond Callahan. 'Servants of the Raj: The Jacob Family in India, 1817-1926'. *Journal of the Society for Army Historical Research* 56, 225 (Spring 1978), pp. 4-24. |

Chaudhuri 1966.         Nirad C. Chaudhuri. *The Continent of Circe*. Bombay, 1966.

Chisholm 1883.         R. F. Chisholm. 'New College for the Gaekwar of Baroda, with Notes on Style and Domical Construction in India'. RIBA *Transactions 1882-83* pp. 141–46.

Clarke 1884.         C. Purdon Clarke. 'Street Architecture of India'. *Journal of the Royal Society of Arts* 32 (1884), pp. 779-88.

Conner 1979.         Patrick Conner. *Oriental Architecture in the West*. London, 1979.

Coomaraswamy 1985.     Ananda K. Coomaraswamy. 'Indian Images with Many Arms'. *The Dance of Siva*. New York, 1985. Pp. 67-71. Originally pub. London, 1924.

Cooper 1986.         Ilay Cooper. 'The Painted Walls of Churu, Jhunjhunu and Sikar Districts of Rajasthan'. *South Asian Studies* 2 (1986), pp. 54-64.

Cooper 1987.         Idem. *Rajasthan: The Guide to Painted Towns of Shekhawati and Churu*. Churu, 1987.

Correa 1987.         Charles Correa. 'Transfers and Transformations'. *Charles Correa*. Ed. by Hasan-Uddin Khan. Rev. ed.: Singapore and Ahmedabad, 1987.

Cruickshank 1987.      Dan Cruickshank. 'Variations and Traditions'. *The Architectural Review* 182, 1086 (Aug. 1987), pp. 50-61.

Curtis 1987.         William J. R. Curtis. 'Modernism and the Search for Indian Identity'. *The Architectural Review* 182, 1086 (Aug. 1987), pp. 32-38.

Davies 1985.         Philip Davies. *Splendours of the Raj: British Architecture in India 1660 to 1947*. London, 1985.

De Forest 1885.        Lockwood de Forest. *Indian Domestic Architecture*. Boston, 1885.

Dhama 1956.         B. L. Dhama. *Indian Architecture*. New Delhi, 1956.

Dhamija 1985.        Jasleen Dhamija (ed). *Crafts of Gujarat*. New York, 1985.

Fergusson 1862.       James Fergusson. *History of the Modern Styles of Architecture*. London, 1862.

Fergusson 1910.       Idem. *History of Indian and Eastern Architecture*. Rev. by J. Burgess and R. Phene Spears. 2 vols. London, 1910. Originally pub. 1876.

Fletcher 1948.        Banister Fletcher. *A History of Architecture on the Comparative Method*. 14th ed.: London, 1948. 1st ed.: 1896.

Goetz 1938.         Hermann Goetz. *The Crisis of Indian Civilization in the Eighteenth and Nineteenth Centuries*. Calcutta, 1938.

Goetz 1950.         Idem. *The Art and Architecture of Bikaner State*. Oxford, 1950.

Goetz 1978.         Idem. 'Late Indian Architecture'. *Rajput Art and Architecture*. Ed. by Jyotindra Jain and Jutta Jain-Neubauer. Wiesbaden, 1978. Pp. 167-88. Originally pub. in *Acta Orientala* (1940).

Gradidge 1981.        Roderick Gradidge. *Edwin Lutyens: Architect Laureate*. London, 1981.

Growse 1880.         F. S. Growse. *Mathura: A District Memoir*. 2d ed.: NWP and Oudh, 1880. Originally pub. 2 vols. NWP, 1874.

Growse 1886.         Idem. *Indian Architecture of Today as Exemplified in New Buildings in the Bulandshahr District*. Pt. 2. Benares, 1886.

Gupta 1981.         Narayani Gupta. *Delhi Between Two Empires 1803-1931: Society, Government and Urban Growth*. Delhi, 1981.

Havell 1913/1927.      E. B. Havell. *Indian Architecture: Its Psychology, Structure, and History from the First Muhammadan Invasion to the Present Day*. London, 1913. And 2nd ed.: London, 1927.

| | |
|---|---|
| Head 1985. | Raymond Head. 'Bagshot Park and Indian Crafts'. *Influences in Victorian Art and Architecture*. Ed. by Sarah Macready and F. H. Thompson. London, 1985. Pp. 139-49. |
| Head 1986. | Idem. *The Indian Style*. London, 1986. |
| Head 1988. | Idem. 'Indian Crafts and Western Design from the Seventeenth Century to the Present'. *Journal of the Royal Society of Arts* 136, 5378 (Jan. 1988), pp. 116-31. |
| Hendley 1884. | Thomas H. Hendley. *Memorials of the Jeypore Exhibition 1883*. 4 vols. London, 1884. |
| Hendley 1896a. | Idem. *Handbook of the Jeypore Museum*. Delhi, 1896. |
| Hendley 1896b. | Idem. *Catalogue of the Collections in the Jeypore Museum*. 2 vols. Delhi, 1896. |
| Hodges 1794. | William Hodges. *Travels in India*. 2d ed.: London, 1794. |
| *Imperial Gazetteer* 1908-1909. | *The Imperial Gazetteer of India*. 26 vols. Oxford, 1908-1909. |
| 'Imperialism and Architecture' 1912. | 'Imperialism and Architecture'. *The Builder* 103, 3634 (27 Sept. 1912), pp. 345-46. |
| Irving 1981. | Robert Grant Irving. *Indian Summer: Lutyens, Baker, and Imperial Delhi*. New Haven and London, 1981. |
| Jacob 1890-1913. | Sir Samuel Swinton Jacob. *Jeypore Portfolio of Architectural Details*. 12 pts. London, 1890-1913. |
| Jain and Jain 1935. | Kesharlal Ajmera Jain and Jawarharlal Jain (eds.). *The Jaipur Album*. Jaipur, 1935. |
| Jaipur . . . Records. | Jaipur Government Secretariat Records: Letters between the Executive Engineer and the Secretary to the Council. Rajasthan State Archives, Bikaner. Ser. no. 256. |
| *Jeypore State Public Works Reports* 1868-1919. | *Jeypore State Public Works Reports* 1886-1919. Calcutta, 1869-1901; Allahabad, 1902-21. |
| Kagal 1986. | Carmen Kagal (ed.) *Vistara, The Architecture of India*. Bombay, 1986. |
| J. L. Kipling 1886. | John Lockwood Kipling. 'Indian Architecture of Today'. *The Journal of Indian Art* 1, 3 (1886), pp. 1-5. |
| R. Kipling 1907. | Rudyard Kipling. *From Sea to Sea*. 2 vols. New York, 1907. |
| Koch 1988. | Ebba Koch. *Shah Jahan and Orpheus: The Pietre Dure Decoration and the Programme of the Throne in the Hall of Public Audiences at the Red Fort of Delhi*. Graz, 1988. |
| Lanchester 1923. | H. V. Lanchester. 'Architecture and Architects in India'. *The Journal of the Royal Institute of British Architects* 30, 10 (Mar. 1923), pp. 293-308. |
| Laurie 1888. | Col. W. F. B. Laurie. *Sketches of Some Distinguished Anglo-Indians*. 2d ser.: London, 1888. |
| Llewellyn-Jones 1985. | Rosie Llewellyn-Jones. *A Fatal Friendship: The Nawabs, the British and the City of Lucknow*. Oxford, 1985. |
| E. Lutyens 1931. | Sir Edwin Lutyens. 'What I Think of Modern Architecture'. *Country Life* 69 (20 June 1931), pp. 775-77. |
| E. Lutyens 1933. | Idem. 'Persian Brickwork – II'. *Country Life* 73 (4 Feb. 1933), pp. 118-23. |
| M. Lutyens 1980. | Mary Lutyens. *Edwin Lutyens*. London, 1980. |

Maffey 1903.        J. L. Maffey. *A Monograph on Wood Carving in the United Provinces of Agra and Oudh*. Allahabad, 1903.

Meade 1987.        Martin Meade. 'Europe in India'. *The Architectural Review* 182, 1086 (Aug. 1987), pp. 26-31.

Metcalf 1984.        Thomas R. Metcalf, 'Architecture and the Representation of Empire: India 1860-1910'. *Representations* 6 (Spring 1984), pp. 37-65.

Mitter 1977.        Partha Mitter. *Much Maligned Monsters: History of European Reactions to Indian Art*. Oxford, 1977.

Moorhouse 1983.        Geoffrey Moorhouse. *India Britannica*. London, 1983.

Morris 1986.        Jan Morris. *Stones of Empire: The Buildings of the Raj*. 2d ed.: Oxford, 1986. Originally pub. 1983.

Naipaul 1977.        V. S. Naipaul. *India: A Wounded Civilization*. London, 1977.

A. Nath 1984.        Aman Nath. 'The Changing Marwari Genius'. *The India Magazine* 4, 4 (Mar. 1984), pp. 56-67.

A. Nath 1986.        Idem. 'Blue Ceramics'. *The India Magazine* 7, 1 (Dec. 1986), pp. 32-43.

A. Nath and Wacziarg 1982.        Idem and Francis Wacziarg. *Rajasthan: The Painted Walls of Shekhavati*. New Delhi, 1982.

A. Nath and Wacziarg 1987.        Idem (eds). *Arts and Crafts of Rajasthan*. London, 1987.

R. Nath 1979.        Ahmad Khan Saiyid. *Monuments of Delhi*. Trans. by R. Nath. New Delhi, 1979. Originally pub. as *Atharal Sanadid*, 1846.

Nevill 1903.        H. R. Nevill. *Bulandshahr: A Gazetteer* (District Gazetteers of the United Provinces of Agra and Oudh 5). Allahabad, 1903.

Nilsson 1968.        Sten Nilsson. *European Architecture in India 1750-1850*. London, 1968.

*Parliamentary Debates* 1912-13.        *The Parliamentary Debates*. 5th ser., vols. 11, 41-56 (1912-13).

Pethe 1987.        Prakash Pethe. 'Indian Architecture – Quest for Identity'. *Architects Trade Journal* 17, 5/6 (May-June 1987), pp. 17-20.

Prasad 1987.        Sunand Prasad. 'Le Corbusier in India'. *Le Corbusier: Architect of the Century*. Exh. cat. London, 1987. Pp. 278-337.

Rahman 1973.        A. Rahman. 'Sixteenth- and Seventeenth-Century Science in India and Some Problems of Comparative Studies'. *Changing Perspectives in the History of Science: Essays in Honour and Joseph Needham*. Ed. by M. Teich and R. Young. London, 1973.

Rewal 1985.        Raj Rewal et al. (eds.). *Architecture in India*. Paris, 1985.

Roy 1978.        Ashim Kumar Roy. *History of the Jaipur City*. New Delhi, 1978.

Ruskin 1903-1912.        John Ruskin. 'The Two Paths'. *The Works of John Ruskin*. Ed. by E. T. Cook and Alexander Wedderburn. London, 1903-12. Vol. 16, pp. 260-310.

Sahai 1986a.        Yaduendra Sahai. 'Princes Planned Eton'. *The Times of India*, 11 Apr., 1986, p. 7.

Sahai 1986b.        Idem. 'All Saints' Church – a Landmark'. *The Times of India*, 25 Dec. 1986, p. 3.

Said 1987.        Edward W. Said. *Orientalism*. Repr.: London, 1987. First pub. 1978.

Sanderson 1913.        Gordon Sanderson. *Types of Modern Indian Buildings*. Allahabad, 1913. Intro. by John Begg.

| | |
|---|---|
| Sarkar 1984. | Jadunath Sarkar. *A History of Jaipur c. 1503-1938*. Ed. by Raghubir Sinh. Hyderabad, 1984. |
| Scherr 1987. | Richard Scherr. 'Uttam Jain: A Modernism Rooted in Tradition'. *Indian Architect and Builder* 1, 2 (Sept. 1987), pp. 6-21. |
| Sehgal 1972. | K. K. Sehgal. *Bikaner* (Rahjasthan District Gazetteers). Jaipur, 1972. |
| Sen 1878. | Opendro Nauth Sen. *Report of the Jeypore School of Arts, for the year ending 31 December 1877. Jaipur, 1878.* |
| Sharar 1975. | Abdul Halim Sharar. *Lucknow: The Last Phase of an Oriental Culture*. Ed. by E. S. Harcourt and F. Hussain. London, 1975. |
| Sharma 1980. | Nandkishore Sharma. *Golden Town. Jaisalmer*. Jaisalmer, 1980. |
| Shils 1961. | Edward Shils. *The Intellectual Between Tradition and Modernity: The Indian Situation*. The Hague, 1961. |
| Shoosmith 1938. | A. G. Shoosmith. 'Present-Day Architecture in India'. *The Nineteenth Century and After* 123 (1938), pp. 204-13. |
| Showers 1916. | H. L. Showers. *Notes on Jaipur*. 2d ed.: Jaipur, 1916. |
| Sleeman 1844. | W. H. Sleeman. *Rambles and Recollections of an Indian Official*. 2 vols. London, 1844. |
| Spear 1984. | Percival Spear. *A History of India*. Vol. 2. 2d ed.: Harmondsworth, 1984. Originally pub. 1965. |
| Srivastava 1981. | Vijai Shankar Srivastava. 'Junagadha Fort, Bikaner'. *Son of the Soil: Maharaja Ganga Singh*. Ed. by Y. P. Singh. Bikaner, 1981. Pp. 225-28. |
| Stamp 1976. | Gavin Stamp. 'Indian Summer'. *The Architectural Review* 159, 952 (June 1976), pp. 365-72. |
| Stamp 1981. | Idem. 'British Architecture in India 1857-1947'. *Journal of the Royal Society of Arts* 129 (May 1981), pp. 357-79. |
| Tandan 1978. | Banmali Tandan. 'The Architecture of the Nawabs of Avadh between 1722 and 1856. A.D. – A Descriptive Inventory and Analysis of Types'. Ph.D. Thesis. Cambridge University, 1978. |
| Tarapor 1982. | Mahrukh Tarapor. 'Growse in Bulandshahr'. *The Architectural Review* 172, 1027 (Sept. 1982), pp. 44-52. |
| Tillotson 1986. | G. H. R. Tillotson. 'Politics and the Taj Mahal'. *Oriental Art* 32, 3 (Autumn 1986), pp. 266-69. |
| Tillotson 1987a. | Idem. *The Rajput Palaces: The Development of an Architectural Style, 1450-1750*. New Haven and London, 1987. |
| Tillotson 1987b. | Idem. *Fan Kwae Pictures: Paintings and Drawings by George Chinnery and Other Artist in the Collection of the Hongkong and Shanghai Banking Corporation*. London, 1987. |
| Tod 1972. | Lt. Col. James Tod. *Annals and Antiquities of Rajast'han*. 2 vols. Repr.: London, 1972. Originally pub. London, 1829/32. |
| Trevelyan 1876. | G. O. Trevelyan. *The Life and Letters of Lord Macaulay*. 2 vols. London, 1876. |
| Villiers-Stuart 1913. | C. M. Villiers-Stuart. *Gardens of the Great Mughals*. London, 1913. |
| Watkin 1977. | David Watkin. *Morality and Architecture*. Oxford, 1977. |
| Watson 1979. | Francis Watson. *A Concise History of India*. London, 1876. |
| Watt 1903. | Sir George Watt. *Indian Art at Delhi 1903*. Calcutta, 1903. |

# Index

# Index